Planning, Implementing, and Maintaining a Microsoft® Windows Server™ 2003 Active Directory Infrastucture (70-294)

Lab Manual

Kurt Hudson

PUBLISHED BY
Microsoft Press
A Division of Microsoft Corporation
One Microsoft Way
Redmond, Washington 98052-6399

Copyright © 2004 by Microsoft Corporation

All rights reserved. No part of the contents of this book may be reproduced or transmitted in any form or by any means without the written permission of the publisher.

Printed and bound in the United States of America.

1 2 3 4 5 6 7 8 9   QWT   8 7 6 5 4 3

A CIP catalogue record for this book is available from the British Library.

Microsoft Press books are available through booksellers and distributors worldwide. For further information about international editions, contact your local Microsoft Corporation office or contact Microsoft Press International directly at fax (425) 936-7329. Visit our Web site at www.microsoft.com/learning. Send comments to *moac@microsoft.com*.

Active Directory, Excel, Exchange, Microsoft, Microsoft Press, MSDN, PowerPoint, Windows, the Windows logo, Windows NT, and Windows Server are either registered trademarks or trademarks of Microsoft Corporation in the United States and/or other countries. Other product and company names mentioned herein may be the trademarks of their respective owners.

The example companies, organizations, products, domain names, e-mail addresses, logos, people, places, and events depicted herein are fictitious. No association with any real company, organization, product, domain name, e-mail address, logo, person, place, or event is intended or should be inferred.

This book expresses the author's views and opinions. The information contained in this book is provided without any express, statutory, or implied warranties. Neither the authors, Microsoft Corporation, nor its resellers or distributors will be held liable for any damages caused or alleged to be caused either directly or indirectly by this book.

Program Manager: Linda Engelman
Project Editor: Lynn Finnel
Technical Editor: Robert Lyon

ISBN 13: 978-0-470-64120-0

SubAssy Part No. X10-36043
Body Part No. X10-23973

TABLE OF CONTENTS

LAB 1: **Exploring Active Directory Domain Membership** 1

    Scenario. 1
    Exercise 1-1: Search Options 2
    Exercise 1-2: Configuring Computers as Domain Members 3
    Exercise 1-3: Finding Domain Resources. 4
        Locating Computers on the Network 4
        Finding a Printer in the Directory. 5
    Exercise 1-4: DNS Client Configuration 6
        Verify Connectivity to the Domain 6
        Causing a Configuration Issue 7
        Testing Connectivity to the Domain 7
        Fix the Client's DNS Issue 8
    Lab Review Questions 8
    Lab Challenge 1-1: Adding an Alternate DNS Server. 8
    Lab Challenge 1-2: Verifying SRV Records 9

LAB 2: **Installing Active Directory** 11

    Scenario. 11
    Lab Dependencies 12
    Exercise 2-1: Installing a Forest and Domain 12
    Exercise 2-2: Verifying SRV Record Creation 14
    Exercise 2-3: Configuring the Even# Computer. 14
        Changing Domain Membership. 14
        Verifying the LDAP SRV Record for the Domain. 16
    Exercise 2-4: Installing a Child Domain 16
    Exercise 2-5: Verifying Child LDAP SRV Records. 18
        Verifying LDAP Record for Child Domain Using DNS Console ... 18
        Verifying LDAP Record for Child Domain Using Nslookup. 19
    Lab Review Questions 19
    Lab Challenge 2-1: Verifying the Kerberos SRV Record
    Exists for the Child Domain 20
    Lab Challenge 2-2: Automating the Installation of a Child Domain .. 20

LAB 3: **Working with Active Directory Sites.** 21

    Scenario. 21
    Lab Dependencies 22
    Exercise 3-1: Replication Management 22
        Forcing Replication 22
        Managing Connection Objects 23

Identifying the Global Catalog. 24
Installing Windows Support Tools 24
Using Repadmin 25
Using Replication Monitor 25
Exercise 3-2: Preparing Your Infrastructure 27
Preparing odd# Computers for Sites. 27
Preparing even# Computers for Sites 28
Restarting odd# and even# Computers. 29
Exercise 3-3: Configuring a Site 29
Creating a Site for odd# Computers 29
Creating a Site for even# Computers and Renaming the
Default-First-Site-Name 29
Exercise 3-4: Configuring a New Subnet 30
Even# Computer Subnet Creation. 30
Odd# Computer Subnet Creation 30
Exercise 3-5: Moving Computers and Creating Site Links 31
Moving the odd# and even# Computer to the Appropriate Site . 31
Creating a Site Link from the even# Computer. 32
Creating a Site Link from the odd# Computer 32
Verifying Replication 33
Lab Review Questions 33
Lab Challenge 3-1: Configuring Preferred Bridgehead
Server for Sites. 34
Lab Challenge 3-2: Making the even# Computer a
Global Catalog Server 34
Post-Lab Cleanup 34

LAB 4: Global Catalog and Flexible Single Master Operations (FSMO) Roles. 37
Lab Dependencies 38
Exercise 4-1: Global Catalog and the Mixed Functional
Level Domain 38
Verifying the Global Catalog is Operational 39
Verifying Functional Levels 39
Adding Experimental User Accounts to the Parent Domain 40
Adding Experimental User Accounts to the Child Domain 41
Allowing Users to Log On to Domain Controllers 42
Simulating a Global Catalog Failure. 42
Logging On Using UPNs for User Accounts 43
Exercise 4-2: Global Catalog and the Native Functional
Level Domain 43
Raising Parent Domain Functional Level 43
Raising Child Domain Functional Level 44

Discovering a Logon Issue 44
Resolving the Global Catalog Outage 44
Logging On to the Child Domain 45
Exercise 4-3: Enabling Universal Group Membership Caching 45
Enabling Universal Group Membership Caching 46
Logging On With Universal Group Membership
Caching Enabled 46
Simulating a Global Catalog Failure. 46
Testing User Logon Without the Global Catalog 47
Exercise 4-4: Working with Flexible Single Master
Operations Roles 47
Viewing Operations Masters. 47
Transferring the Schema Master to a Different
Domain Controller 48
Transferring the Schema Master to the New Server 49
Lab Review Questions 49
Lab Challenge 4-1: Using the DNS Console to Verify
Global Catalog Records on the DNS Server 50
Lab Challenge 4-2: Verifying FSMO Role Holders with DCDiag. 50
Lab Challenge 4-3: Determining Whether an Attribute Is Replicated
in the Global Catalog. 50

Troubleshooting Lab A 51
Reviewing A Network 51
Troubleshooting A Break Scenario. 52
Break Scenario 1 53
Break Scenario 2 54

LAB 5: **Creating and Managing Users and Groups** 55
Lab Dependencies 56
Exercise 5-1: Creating Administrative Accounts 57
Creating Administrative Accounts on the Parent Domains 57
Creating Administrative Accounts on the Child Domain. 58
Adding Child User Accounts to Enterprise-Wide
Administrative Roles 59
Exercise 5-2: Testing Administrative Access 60
Which Accounts Can Create Sites? 60
Which Accounts Can Create Users? 61
Which Accounts Can Manage the Schema? 62
Exercise 5-3: Configuring Groups and Permissions. 64
Creating Global Groups 64
Creating Universal Groups 65
Assigning Permissions Through Group Membership 66
Exercise 5-4: Using dsadd to Add a User Account 66

Using dsadd to Create an OU and User in the Parent Domain . . 66
Using dsadd to Create an OU and User in the Child Domain . . . 67
Lab Review Questions 67
Lab Challenge 5-1: Using DSADD to Add a User Account to the
Users Container 68
Lab Challenge 5-2: Changing the UPN Suffix with LDIFDE 68

LAB 6: Employing Security Concepts. 69

Lab Dependencies 70
Exercise 6-1: Using Naming Standards
and Secure Passwords 70
Creating User Accounts with Alternate Character
Passwords on Both Domains 71
Exercise 6-2: Employing Administrator Account Security 72
Using Runas at the Command Prompt Window 72
Using Runas from the Run Dialog Box. 73
Creating and Using a Runas Shortcut 73
Attempting to Run Multiple Runas Consoles Simultaneously. . . 73
Exercise 6-3: Delegating Administrative Responsibility 74
Delegating Control on the Parent Domain 74
Delegating Control on the Child Domain 75
Testing Delegated Permissions on the Parent Domain 77
Testing Delegated Permissions on the Child Domain 77
Exercise 6-4: HIDING A User Account 78
Finding a User in Active Directory from the Parent Domain 78
Finding a User in Active Directory from the Child Domain 79
Resetting Permission for Mgmt1. 79
Resetting Permission for Mgmt2. 80
Finding a User in Active Directory from the Parent Domain 81
Finding a User in Active Directory from the Child Domain 82
Lab Review Questions 82
Lab Challenge 6-1: Using DSMOVE 82
Lab Challenge 6-2: Moving An OU with Movetree 83
Lab Challenge 6-3: Moving A User With Movetree 83

LAB 7: Exploring Group Policy Adminstration 85

Scenario. 85
Lab Dependencies 86
Exercise 7-1: Configuring the Local Computer Policy. 87
Exercise 7-2: Processing Order. 88
Configure the Remove Run Policy Setting on the Domain 88
Verify Domain GPO Overrides Local Computer Policy. 89
Exercise 7-3: Priority Order. 91
Another GPO for L7Test1 91

Exercise 7-4: Block Policy Inheritance and No Override.......... 93
Exercise 7-5: Using User Group Policy Loopback Processing Mode . 95
Lab Review Questions.................................. 96
Lab Challenge 7-1: Disabling the Shutdown Event Tracker 97
Lab Challenge 7-2: Hiding Last Logged On User Name.......... 97
Post-Lab Cleanup 97

LAB 8: Managing Users and Computers with Group Policy 99
Scenario.. 99
Lab Dependencies 100
Exercise 8-1: Account Policies 100
    Adjusting the Account Lockout Policy:................. 103
Exercise 8-2: Audit Policies 104
Exercise 8-3: Folder Redirection 107
Exercise 8-4: Disk Quotas 109
Lab Review Questions.................................. 111
Lab Challenge 8-1: Managing the Password Policy 111
Lab Challenge 8-2: Configuring the Account Lockout Policy...... 112
Post-Lab Cleanup 112

Troubleshooting Lab B 115
Reviewing a Network 115
Troubleshooting A Break Scenario........................ 118
    Break Scenario 1 118
    Break Scenario 2 119

LAB 9: Software Distribution..................... 121
Scenario.. 121
Lab Dependencies 122
Exercise 9-1: Deploying Software to Users 122
Exercise 9-2: Using Software Restriction Policies............. 126
Exercise 9-3: Deploying Software to Computers.............. 128
Lab Review Questions.................................. 130
Lab Challenge 9-1: Deploying Administrative Tools............ 130
Lab Challenge 9-2: Restricting Access to CMD 130
Post-Lab Cleanup 130

LAB 10: Controlling Group Policy.................... 133
Scenario.. 133
Lab Dependencies 134
Exercise 10-1: GPRESULT and RSOP...................... 135
Exercise 10-2: Using Security Filtering 138
Exercise 10-3: Working with WMI Filters 141
Lab Review Questions.................................. 143
Lab Challenge 10-1: Applying Security Filtering 144

CONTENTS

  Lab Challenge 10-2: Applying WMI Filtering 144
  Post-Lab Cleanup 144

LAB 11: Disaster Recovery and Maintenance 147
  Lab Dependencies 148
  Exercise 11-1: Replica Domain Controller 148
  Exercise 11-2: Resolving Replication Issues 149
  Exercise 11-3: System State Data Backup 152
  Exercise 11-4: Compacting the Database 154
  Exercise 11-5: Authoritative Restore 156
  Lab Review Questions 159
  Lab Challenge 11-1: Restoring a User Account 159
  Post-Lab Cleanup 159

LAB 12: Integration and Migration 161
  Lab Dependencies 162
  Exercise 12-1: Installing a New Forest 162
  Exercise 12-2: Creating Cross-Forest Trusts 164
  Exercise 12-3: Using Activer Directory Migration Tool
  to Migrate Users 168
  Lab Review Questions 174
  Lab Challenge 12-1: Migrating Users Between Forests 175
  Lab Challenge 12-2: Migrating Computers Between Forests 175

Troubleshooting Lab C 177
  Reviewing A Network 177
  Troubleshooting A Break Scenario. 178
    Break Scenario 1 178
    Break Scenario 2 180

LAB 1
EXPLORING ACTIVE DIRECTORY DOMAIN MEMBERSHIP

This lab contains the following exercises and activities:

- Exercise 1-1: Search Options
- Exercise 1-2: Configuring Computers as Domain Members
- Exercise 1-3: Finding Domain Resources
- Exercise 1-4: DNS Client Configuration
- Lab Review Questions
- Lab Challenge 1-1: Adding an Alternate DNS Server
- Lab Challenge 1-2: Verifying SRV Records

SCENARIO

You are a network support specialist for Contoso, Limited. Contoso has a large single domain network. You are responsible for helping users connect to domain resources. Contoso recently implemented the contoso.com Active Directory domain. Because many of the computers are not yet members of this domain, your current duties involve the following:

- Assist users to locate resources; some users are configured to use the domain and others are not.
- Configure existing computers as members of the new domain.
- Resolve issues that prevent network users from connecting to domain resources.

NOTE In this lab you will see the characters **zz**. When you see these characters, substitute the two-digit number assigned to your computer. Whenever you see the Manage Your Server page appear in this lab, select the Don't Display This Page At Logon check box and close the Manage Your Server page.

After completing this lab, you will be able to:

- Configure Domain Name System (DNS) client settings to contact an Active Directory domain controller.
- Demonstrate the differences between domain and nondomain member computer search and logon options.
- Add a computer to a domain.
- Resolve DNS name resolution issues.
- Verify the creation of service resource (SRV) records.

Estimated lesson time: 105 minutes

EXERCISE 1-1: SEARCH OPTIONS

Estimated completion time: 10 minutes

A network user is trying to locate resources on the domain. The network user is having some difficulty finding domain resources.

Since your computer is not configured as a domain member right now, you can use this opportunity to view the type of search options that are available to a computer in a workgroup. Later, you'll investigate how a domain member's search options are different.

1. Press Ctrl+Alt+Delete and log on as the default administrator of the local computer. Your username will be **Administrator**. The password will be **MSPress#1** or the password your instructor or lab proctor assigns to you.

2. Click Start, and then click Search to open the Search Results window.
3. Expand the Search Results window to full screen if necessary.
4. Click Other Search Options in the left window pane.
5. Click Computers Or People in the left window pane.

   QUESTION What search options do you see in the left window pane?

6. Click the A Computer On The Network search option.
7. In the Computer Name text box in the left window pane, type **Instructor01**.
8. Click the Search button.

   QUESTION What search results do you see in the right window pane?

9. Close the Search Results window.

EXERCISE 1-2: CONFIGURING COMPUTERS AS DOMAIN MEMBERS

Estimated completion time: 20 minutes

Your manager assigns you the task of configuring the computers on the network as members of the domain. To begin, you must configure your own computer as a member of the domain.

1. Click Start, right-click My Computer, and then click Properties on the shortcut menu. The System Properties dialog box opens.
2. Click the Computer Name tab.
3. Click the Change button. The Computer Name Changes dialog box opens.

   QUESTION What do you see as the computer name?

4. Click the More button. The DNS Suffix And NetBIOS Computer Name dialog box appears.

   QUESTION Is the NetBIOS name of your computer the same as your computer name?

   QUESTION Can you change the NetBIOS computer name on this screen?

5. In the Primary DNS Suffix Of This Computer text box, type **contoso.com**, and click OK.
6. In the Member Of section of the dialog box, click the Domain option button. Type the domain name **contoso.com**, and click OK. The Computer Name Changes dialog box appears.
7. Type the name **Administrator**, and password **MSPress#1**, and click OK. You should see an error message.

   QUESTION Why are the user name and password for your local administrator account not able to join you to the domain?

8. Click OK on the error message.
9. Click OK in the Computer Name Changes dialog box to try again. The Computer Name Changes dialog box appears.
10. Type the name **studentzz**, Enter a password of **MSPress#1**.
11. Click OK. You should see a Welcome To The Contoso.com Domain message.
12. Click OK. Another Computer Name Changes dialog box appears informing you that the computer must be restarted in order for the changes to take effect.
13. Click OK to confirm the restart message.
14. Click OK in the System Properties dialog box.

LAB 1: EXPLORING ACTIVE DIRECTORY DOMAIN MEMBERSHIP

15. The System Settings Change dialog box appears asking if you'd like to restart your computer now. Click Yes to restart the computer.

16. When the computer restarts, press Ctrl+Alt+Delete and you'll see the Welcome to Windows Logon dialog box. Click Options. The Log On To selection box appears.

17. Select CONTOSO from the selection box.

QUESTION *Why are you presented with this choice to log on to COMPUTERzz or CONTOSO? What is the difference?*

18. In the User Name box, type **studentzz**. Enter a password of **MSPress#1**, and click OK.

    NOTE *If you see a product activation warning, click OK. You can click Start, select All Programs, and then select Activate Windows in order to activate the product. Activate the product only if requested by your instructor or lab supervisor.*

19. Log off of the computer.

EXERCISE 1-3: FINDING DOMAIN RESOURCES

Estimated completion time: 15 minutes

A network user asks you to help him find the domain controller and a printer on the domain. You must help this user to find these resources on the network.

Locating Computers on the Network

In this activity, you'll use the search option to locate the domain controller named Instructor01.

1. Log on as **studentzz** of the contoso domain, and the password **MSPress#1**.

2. Open the Search Results window.

3. Expand the Search Results window to full screen if necessary.

4. Click Other Search Options in the left window pane.

   QUESTION Are there any extra features to search on the Computers And People search option?

5. Click Printers, Computers Or People in the left window pane.
6. Click the A Computer On The Network search option in the left window pane.
7. In the Computer Name text box in the left window pane, type **Instructor01**.
8. Click the Search button in the left window pane.

   QUESTION Compare your results from Exercise 1-1. Are the results different? If so, what is the difference?

9. Close the window.

Finding a Printer in the Directory

In this activity, you'll use the search option to locate a printer that has *WA* as part of its location.

1. Open the Search Results window.
2. Expand the Search Results window to full screen if necessary.
3. Click Other Search Options in the left window pane.
4. Click Printers, Computers, Or People and then click A Printer On The Network in the left window pane.
5. A Find Printers dialog box should open. Expand the Find Printers dialog box if necessary. Notice that there is an In selection box, which has Entire Directory selected.
6. Click the drop-down selection box where you see Entire Directory. Inside the selection box, you see two options listed.

   QUESTION What are these options and what is the difference between them?

7. Select Contoso from the listed options.
8. Click the text box named Location. Type **WA** for the location.
9. Click Find Now.
10. Record the search results in a screen capture.

    NOTE Refer to the ScreenCaptureDirections.doc file to learn how to take a screen capture, if you are uncertain. This file should be located in your C:\Lab Manual\Lab01 folder.

11. Close all open windows.
12. Log off of the computer.

EXERCISE 1-4: DNS CLIENT CONFIGURATION

Estimated completion time: 20 minutes

You are trying to resolve a client connectivity issue. The client computer is not able to ping the domain or make a connection to any domain resources.

In this exercise you will create a DNS problem for a client computer and then repair it. First, you'll verify that your computer is able to receive a ping response from the contoso.com domain. Then you'll change your Preferred DNS server settings to your own IP address to see how this causes a problem. After that, you'll fix your Preferred DNS server.

Verify Connectivity to the Domain

In this activity, you'll ensure that you are able to receive a ping response from the contoso.com domain.

1. Log on as the default administrator of the local computer.

2. Open a command prompt window.

   NOTE *To open a command prompt window, click Start, and then click Run. Type* **CMD** *in the Open text box, and click OK.*

3. Expand the command prompt window if necessary.

4. Type **ipconfig /all > c:\ipconfig.txt** in the command prompt window, and press ENTER. You may now open this document in Notepad to show your IP Configuration Information. Here is sample information from Computer02.

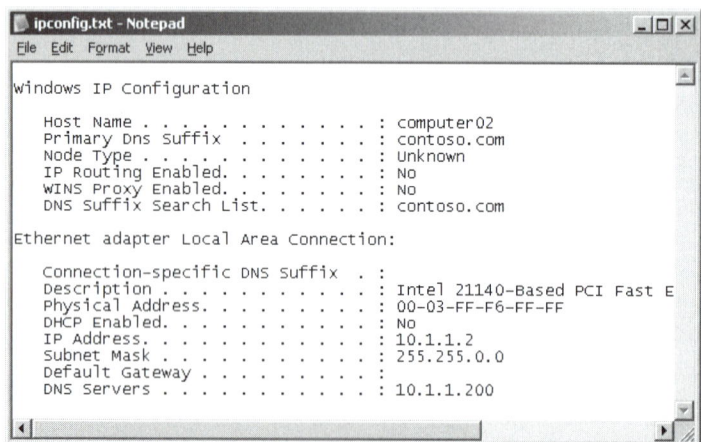

5. Use the ping utility to test connectivity to contoso.com. To ping contoso.com, type **ping contoso.com** in the command prompt window, and press ENTER.

   QUESTION *How many packets were sent, received, and lost?*

Causing a Configuration Issue

In this activity, you'll incorrectly configure your Preferred DNS server settings.

1. Click Start, click Control Panel, and then click Network Connections. Right-click Local Area Connection, and then click Properties. The Local Area Connection Properties dialog box opens.

2. Select Internet Protocol (TCP/IP), and then click Properties. The Internet Protocol (TCP/IP) Properties dialog box opens.

3. In the Preferred DNS Server text box, enter the IP address as shown in the IP Address text box in the upper part of the dialog box. Here are the settings for Computer02.

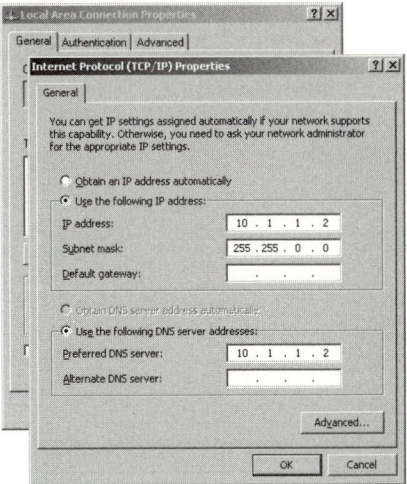

4. Click OK.
5. Click Close In The Local Area Connection Properties dialog box.
6. Log off of the computer.

Testing Connectivity to the Domain

In this activity, you'll attempt to log on to the domain and receive a ping response from contoso.com.

1. Log on as **studentzz** of the Contoso domain.
2. Open a command prompt window.
3. Ping contoso.com.

    QUESTION Was the ping successful? Why or why not?

4. Ping Instructor01.

    QUESTION Was the ping successful? Why or why not?

Fix the Client's DNS Issue

In this activity, you'll repair the client's DNS issue by configuring the proper DNS server.

1. Log off of the domain and log on as the default administrator of the local computer.
2. Set the Preferred DNS server back to the original settings.

   NOTE The original Preferred DNS server information can be found in the Ipconfig.txt file on your C drive. Use Notepad to view the file.

3. Open a command prompt window.
4. Ping contoso.com. Verify that four packets were sent, four packets were received, and none were lost.
5. Close all open windows.

   QUESTION Why was the student domain account able to log on when the DNS settings were incorrect?

LAB REVIEW QUESTIONS

Estimated completion time: 15 minutes

1. In your words, describe what you learned during this lab.
2. If cached credentials were disabled on your domain through Group Policies, what additional consequences could you expect an improperly configured DNS client to possibly add?
3. How do the search options of a client computer that is a member of a domain vary from those of a client computer that is not connected to a domain?
4. In order to add a computer to a domain, what group membership must you have?
5. If there is a domain controller on your network named DC1 with IP address 192.168.1.1, and you issue a ping DC1 command with zero returned packets, what might you try next? If a ping to 192.168.1.1 was successful, what would you suspect is the problem?

LAB CHALLENGE 1-1: ADDING AN ALTERNATE DNS SERVER

Estimated completion time: 15 minutes

Your manager just finished installing a second DNS server for your network. You must configure your server computer to utilize this DNS server in the event that the primary DNS server fails. A custom application also requires you to reference this server by the name *altdns*.

To complete this lab challenge, you'll have to add your computer's IP address as the Alternate DNS server. Make and save a screen capture of your IP configuration when you've completed this procedure. You must also modify the host's file to add the name altdns and map it to your IP address. Verify that the name is added to your cache using the ipconfig command. Also, ping the altdns address and verify that it is working properly.

LAB CHALLENGE 1-2: VERIFYING SRV RECORDS

Estimated completion time: 15 minutes

Your manager just completed the installation of a domain controller. You must verify that the SRV record for the domain controller was properly created in DNS.

Verify that the classroom or lab domain SRV records have been created. Use the NSLookup.exe utility to complete this challenge. Make and save a screen capture of your NSLookup results. (Hint: Directions on verifying the SRV records for a domain can be located in the Windows Server 2003 help file. Search for the key words *NSLookup SRV*.)

LAB 2
INSTALLING ACTIVE DIRECTORY

This lab contains the following exercises and activities:

- Exercise 2-1: Installing a Forest and Domain
- Exercise 2-2: Verifying SRV Record Creation
- Exercise 2-3: Configuring the Even# Computer
- Exercise 2-4: Installing a Child Domain
- Exercise 2-5: Verifying Child LDAP SRV Records
- Lab Review Questions
- Lab Challenge 2-1: Verifying the Kerberos SRV Record Exists for the Child Domain
- Lab Challenge 2-2: Automating the Installation of a Child Domain

SCENARIO

You are the network administrator of Tailspin Toys. You are assigned to install a new forest root for the company. After you complete the installation, you must verify that the installation was successful. Then you must install a child domain in the new forest.

After completing this lab, you will be able to:

- Create an Active Directory forest and domain tree
- Install a child domain and domain controller
- Verify SRV records
- Automate the installation of Active Directory

Estimated lesson time: 115 minutes

NOTE In this lab, you will see the characters **xx**, **yy**, and **zz**. These directions assume that you are working on computers configured in pairs and that each computer has a number. One number is odd and the other number is even. For example, Computer01 is the odd# computer and Computer02 is the even# computer. When you see **xx**, substitute the unique number assigned to the odd# computer. When you see **yy**, substitute the unique number assigned to the even# computer. When you see **zz**, substitute the number assigned to the computer you are working at, either odd or even.

Whenever you see the Manage Your Server page appear in this lab, select the Don't Display This Page At Logon check box and close the Manage Your Server page.

LAB DEPENDENCIES

You must complete Lab 1, Exercise 1-4, in order for this lab to work properly.

EXERCISE 2-1: INSTALLING A FOREST AND DOMAIN

Estimated completion time: 20 minutes

Your manager has assigned you to install Active Directory for your company. You must install the forest root domain controller.

CAUTION This exercise is to be completed only on the odd# computers such as 1, 3, 5, 7, and so on.

In this exercise, you'll install Active Directory on the odd# computers. You'll name your new domain Domain*xx*, and you'll allow Active Directory to install and configure Domain Name System (DNS) automatically.

1. On the odd# computer, log on as the default administrator of the local computer.

2. Run Dcpromo.

    NOTE To run Dcpromo, click Start, click Run, type **Dcpromo**, and press ENTER.

3. The Welcome To The Active Directory Installation Wizard appears. Click Next to proceed with Active Directory installation.

4. On the Operating System Compatibility page, click Next.

5. On the Domain Controller Type page, select Domain Controller For A New Domain, and then click Next.

6. On the Create New Domain page, ensure that Domain In A New Forest is selected, and then click Next.

7. On the New Domain Name page in the Full DNS Name For New Domain box, type **domain*xx*.local**, and then click Next.

8. After a few moments, the NetBIOS Domain Name page appears. Use the default NetBIOS name (DOMAIN*xx*), and then click Next.

9. On the Database And Log Folders page, click Next. This leaves the log files and database in their default location.

10. On the Shared System Volume page, ensure that the Sysvol folder is on a volume formatted with NTFS. (This should already have been done.) Click Next.

11. On the DNS Registration Diagnostics page, view the details of the diagnostic test. Then ensure that the Install And Configure The DNS Server On This Computer And Set This Computer To Use This DNS Server As Its Preferred DNS Server option button is selected, and click Next.

12. On the Permissions page, click Next to accept the default permissions setting.

13. On the Directory Services Restore Mode Administrator Password page, type **MSPress#1** as the restore mode password. Confirm the password by typing it again, and then click Next.

14. Review the Summary dialog box, and then click Next.

15. A message box appears. The message informs you that as part of the Active Directory installation process, this server was disjoined from its domain. However, the computer account for the server was not disabled. A domain administrator can disable or delete the computer account for this server. Click OK to continue.

    You might be asked to insert the Windows Server 2003 CD during the installation.

16. When the Completing The Active Directory Installation Wizard page appears, click Finish, and then click Restart Now to restart the computer.

17. Log on as the default administrator of the domain*xx*.domain and open the Local Area Connection Properties dialog box.

18. Open the Internet Protocol (TPC/IP) Properties dialog box and ensure that the Preferred DNS Server address is set to the same address as the IP Address. If not, change the Prefrred DNS Server box to match the IP Address of the local computer. Example settings for Computer03 are shown in the following figure.

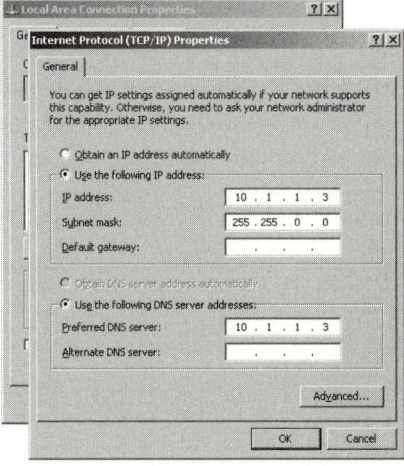

19. Close all open windows. If you changed the Preferred DNS Server address, restart the computer.

EXERCISE 2-2: VERIFYING SRV RECORD CREATION

Estimated completion time: 5 minutes

Your colleague has just completed the installation of a domain controller. Your colleague asks you to verify the **Lightweight Directory Access Protocol (LDAP)** service location (SRV) resource record for the domain controller.

1. Ensure that you are logged on to the computer as the default administrator of the local computer.
2. Open a command prompt window.
3. Type **nslookup** in the command prompt window, and press ENTER.

   NOTE *If you see an error message that says "Can't find server name for address," which is followed by the IP address of your DNS server, this means that your DNS server doesn't have a reverse lookup zone. Do not worry about this error, but for more information see the following Knowledge Base articles: 172953 titled "How to Install and Configure Microsoft DNS Server" and 242906 titled "'DNS Request Timed Out' Error Message When you Start Nslookup From a Command Line"*

4. Type **set type=srv** and press ENTER.
5. Type **_ldap._tcp.dc._msdcs.domain.xx.local** and press ENTER. If you are working at the odd# computer, the LDAP SRV resource record for the domain controller of your domain is displayed. If you are working at the even# computer, an error message is displayed. The error message indicates that the lookup operation timed out or the domain is non-existent.

   QUESTION *Why does the even# computer receive this error message?*

6. Type **exit**, and press ENTER.
7. Close the command prompt window.

EXERCISE 2-3: CONFIGURING THE EVEN# COMPUTER

Estimated completion time: 10 minutes

Your manager asks you to verify the **Lightweight Directory Access Protocol (LDAP)** service location (SRV) resource record of a new domain she just created. She tells you to use a computer that is already a member of a different domain. You must configure the computer as a member of the domain that your manager just created.

   CAUTION *Exercise 2-3 and its subordinate activities should be performed only on the even# computer.*

Changing Domain Membership

In this exercise, you'll configure the even# computer as a member of the odd# computer's domain.

1. Configure the even# computer's Preferred DNS Server to point to the odd# computer's IP address.

    NOTE *You learned how to reconfigure DNS server settings in Lab 1, Exercise 1-4.*

2. Join the odd# computer's domain. Click Start, right-click My Computer, and click Properties from the shortcut menu. The System Properties dialog box opens.

3. Click the Computer Name tab, and click Change. The Computer Name Changes dialog box opens.

    QUESTION *What do you see as the Member Of name?*

4. In the Member Of section of the dialog box, confirm that the Domain option button is selected. Type the domain name **domain*xx*.local**, and click OK.

5. The Computer Name Changes dialog box appears. Enter the **student*zz*** credentials, and click OK.

6. You should see an error message like the one shown in the following figure.

    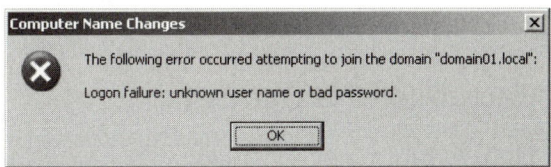

    QUESTION *Why is the user name and password for your student*zz* account not able to join you to the domain?*

7. Click OK on the error message.

8. Click OK in the Computer Name Changes dialog box to try again. Another Computer Name Changes dialog box appears.

9. Enter the administrator credentials. This is the user name and password that was used to install the odd# computer's domain (the user name should be Administrator and the password should be MSPress#1). Then click OK. You should see a Welcome To The domain*xx*.local Domain message.

10. Click OK. A Computer Name Changes dialog box appears informing you that the computer must be restarted in order for the changes to take effect.

11. Click OK to confirm the restart message.

12. Click OK in the System Properties dialog box. The System Settings Change dialog box appears asking if you'd like to restart your computer now.

13. Click Yes to restart the computer. When the computer restarts, press CTRL+ALT+DELETE and, you'll see the Welcome To Windows Logon dialog box.

14. Click Options. The Log On To selection box appears. The following figure shows an example of Computer02 on the domain01 domain.

16 LAB 2: INSTALLING ACTIVE DIRECTORY

15. Select domain*xx* from this selection box. Enter the domain administrator name and password (the user name should be **Administrator** and the password should be **MSPress#1**). Click OK.

    NOTE *The studentzz user accounts have not been created on the new domain controller for the domainxx.local. Attempting to use these accounts to log on to the new domain will fail. When you log on for the rest of these exercises, you should use the domain administrator account, which is the same as your previous local administrator account.*

Verifying the LDAP SRV Record for the Domain

In this exercise, you'll verify the **Lightweight Directory Access Protocol (LDAP)** service location (SRV) resource record of the domain controller in the odd# computer's domain.

1. Open a command prompt window.
2. Type **nslookup** in the command prompt window, and press ENTER.
3. Type **set type=srv**, and press Enter.
4. Type **_ldap._tcp.dc._msdcs.domain.*xx*.local**, and press Enter. A summary output is displayed. The information displayed is showing the LDAP SRV resource record for domain controllers within the domain.
5. Type **exit**, and press ENTER.
6. Close the command prompt window.
7. Log off.

EXERCISE 2-4: INSTALLING A CHILD DOMAIN

Estimated completion time: 20 minutes

Your manager has assigned you to install a child domain for your company's existing domain.

CAUTION *Exercise 2-4 and its subordinate activities should be performed only on the even# computer.*

In this exercise, you'll install the even# computer as a child domain to the odd# computer. For example, if you were working at computer02, you'd install a child domain named child01.domain01.local.

1. On the even# computer, log on as the default administrator of the local computer.

2. Run Dcpromo.

3. The Welcome To The Active Directory Installation Wizard appears. Click Next to proceed with Active Directory installation.

4. On the Operating System Compatibility page, click Next.

5. On the Domain Controller Type page, select Domain Controller For A New Domain, and then click Next.

6. On the Create New Domain page, select Child Domain In An Existing Domain Tree, and then click Next.

7. On the Network Credentials page, type the Administrator credentials, username: **Administrator**, password: **MSPress#1**, or whatever your instructor or lab proctor has assigned to you. Type **domain*xx*.local** in the Domain text box, and click Next.

8. On the Child Domain Installation page in the Parent Domain box, ensure that **domain*xx*.local** is entered. Type **child*xx*** in the Child Domain text box. The following figure is an example of installing Computer02 as a child domain of Computer01. Click Next.

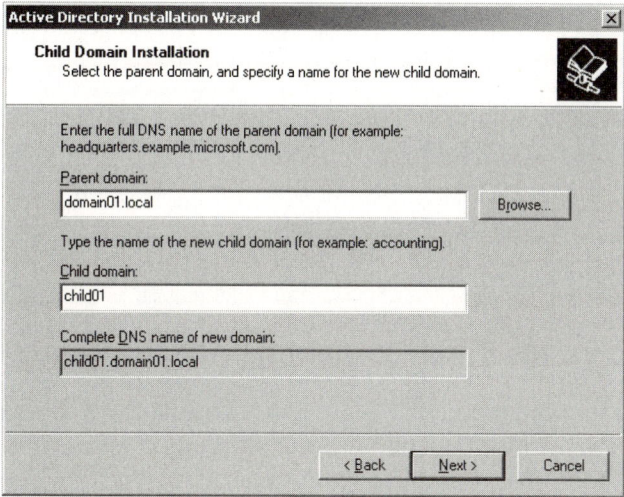

9. After a few moments, the NetBIOS Domain Name page appears. Use the default NetBIOS name (CHILD*XX*), and then click Next.

10. On the Database And Log Folders page, click Next. This leaves the log files and database in their default location.

11. On the Shared System Volume page, ensure that the Sysvol folder is on a volume formatted with NTFS. (This should already have been done.) Click Next.

LAB 2: INSTALLING ACTIVE DIRECTORY

12. On the DNS Registration Diagnostics page, view the details of the diagnostic test. Then ensure that the operation completed successfully.

13. Make and save a screen capture of the DNS Registration Diagnostics page. Then click Next.

    QUESTION What does a successful DNS test indicate?

14. On the Permissions page, click Next to accept the default permissions setting.

15. On the Directory Services Restore Mode Administrator Password page, type **MSPress#1** as the restore mode password. Confirm the password by typing it again, and then click Next to proceed with the Active Directory installation.

16. Review the Summary page, and then click Next to install Active Directory.

17. When the Completing The Active Directory Installation Wizard page appears, click Finish, and then click Restart Now. The computer restarts.

18. Log on as the default administrator of the child*xx* domain.

EXERCISE 2-5: VERIFYING CHILD LDAP SRV RECORDS

Estimated completion time: 5 minutes

Your colleague has just completed the installation of a child domain. Your colleague asks you to verify that the **Lightweight Directory Access Protocol (LDAP)** service location (SRV) resource record was created on the parent domain's DNS server.

- For the student at the odd# computer, complete "Verifying LDAP Record for Child Domain Using DNS Console."

- For the student at the even# computer, complete "Verifying LDAP Record for Child Domain Using Nslookup."

Verifying LDAP Record for Child Domain Using DNS Console

For the student at the odd# computer, you'll verify that a **Lightweight Directory Access Protocol (LDAP)** record for the child domain was added to his or her Domain Name System (DNS) server through the DNS console.

1. On the odd# computer, ensure that you are logged on as the default administrator of the domain*xx* domain.

2. Open the DNS console. Click Start, click Run, and type **dnsmgmt.msc** into the drop-down box.

3. In the left window pane, expand the Forward Lookup Zones, expand the domain*xx*.local branch, expand the child*xx* branch, expand the _msdcs branch, and expand the dc branch. Select the _tcp node.

NOTE Modification: If the childxx branch does not appear in the console tree, try restarting the child domain controller.

4. In the right window pane, select the _ldap record.
5. Make and save a screen capture of the DNS console.

   QUESTION Did you notice anything about the location of the record in the DNS console and the path used in Nslookup to verify the record?

6. Close the DNS console window.

Verifying LDAP Record for Child Domain Using Nslookup

For the student at the even# computer, verify that a **Lightweight Directory Access Protocol (LDAP)** record for the child domain was added to his or her DNS server through the DNS console.

1. On the even# computer, ensure you are logged on as the default administrator of the child*xx* domain.
2. Open a command prompt window.
3. Type **nslookup**, and press ENTER.
4. Type **set type=srv**, and press ENTER.
5. Type **_ldap._tcp.dc._msdcs.child*xx*.domain*xx*.local**, and press ENTER.
6. A summary output is displayed. The information displayed is showing the LDAP SRV resource record for domain controllers within the domain.
7. Type **exit**, and press ENTER.
8. Close the command prompt window.

LAB REVIEW QUESTIONS

Estimated completion time: 10 minutes

1. In your words, describe what you learned during this lab.
2. When a child domain is installed and the parent domain is hosting an Active Directory–integrated DNS server that allows dynamic updates, are the SRV resource records of the child domain added automatically during Active Directory installation?
3. How is a child domain represented in the Domain Name System (DNS) console?
4. Which domain controller establishes the name of the forest?
5. Whether you are installing a child domain or the first domain in a forest, what are some common parameters you define for the Active Directory installation process?

LAB CHALLENGE 2-1: VERIFYING THE KERBEROS SRV RECORD EXISTS FOR THE CHILD DOMAIN

Estimated completion time: 5 minutes

The security administrator for your company wants to know if the Kerberos Key Distribution Center (KDC) record is available for your domain.

Each domain controller registers several service location (SRV) resource records. One of these records identifies the Kerberos KDC, which is also the domain controller. Use Nslookup to verify that this record exists for the child domain.

LAB CHALLENGE 2-2: AUTOMATING THE INSTALLATION OF A CHILD DOMAIN

Estimated completion time: 40 minutes

Your manager wants you to build an Active Directory answer file that can be given to junior network administrators to install child domains at remote sites. You must create and prove that this answer file works. To do so, you'll remove a child domain that you configured in your test lab. Then you'll create an answer file that can be used to reinstall it.

NOTE Hint: To learn how to create this answer file, you should search on the term DCINSTALL and also review Microsoft Knowledge Base article Q223757.

LAB 3
WORKING WITH ACTIVE DIRECTORY SITES

This lab contains the following exercises and activities:
- Exercise 3-1: Replication Management
- Exercise 3-2: Preparing Your Infrastructure
- Exercise 3-3: Configuring a Site
- Exercise 3-4: Configuring a New Subnet
- Exercise 3-5: Moving Computers and Creating Site Links
- Lab Review Questions
- Lab Challenge 3-1: Configuring Preferred Bridgehead Server for Sites
- Lab Challenge 3-2: Making the even# Computer a Global Catalog Server

SCENARIO

You are a network administrator for the contoso.com domain. Contoso.com contains two domain controllers running Microsoft Windows Server 2003, Enterprise Edition. However, you are preparing to install several more domain controllers in the near future as your company expands. These new locations will be across slow wide area network (WAN) links. You must prepare your existing structure to support multiple sites. Before you do this, you must verify your existing site structure. When the remote locations are added, you must add a site for each location. Finally, you must investigate the configuration of additional global catalog servers for the new remote locations.

After completing this lab, you will be able to:
- Use Active Directory Sites And Services, Repadmin, and Replmon to manage Active Directory sites.
- View a replication topology.
- Create Active Directory sites.
- Configure bridgehead servers between sites.
- Configure a global catalog server.

Estimated lesson time: 145 minutes

LAB 3: WORKING WITH ACTIVE DIRECTORY SITES

NOTE In this lab, you will see the characters **xx**, **yy**, and **zz**. These directions assume that you are working on computers configured in pairs and that each computer has a number. One number is odd and the other number is even. For example, Computer01 is the odd# computer and Computer02 is the even# computer. When you see **xx**, substitute the unique number assigned to the odd# computer. When you see **yy**, substitute the unique number assigned to the even# computer. When you see **zz**, substitute the number assigned to the computer you are working at, either odd or even.

Whenever you see the Manage Your Server page appear in this lab, select the Don't Display This Page At Logon check box and close the Manage Your Server page.

LAB DEPENDENCIES

In order to complete this lab, you must be sure that the following is done:

- The even# computer must be configured to use the odd# computer as its Preferred DNS Server, as explained in Lab 1, Exercise 1-4.
- Active Directory is installed on the odd# computer. Lab 2, Exercise 2-1 covers the installation of Active Directory on the odd# computer.
- Active Directory is installed on the even# computer. Lab 2, Exercises 2-3 and 2-4 cover the installation of Active Directory on the even# computer.

EXERCISE 3-1: REPLICATION MANAGEMENT

Estimated completion time: 60 minutes

You want to verify that the domain controllers in your site are replicating information properly. You've reviewed the replication error messages in the Event Viewer Directory Service log to find those that you are anxious to resolve. First, you plan to force replication. Then you plan to create a manual connection object. After that, you'll use Repadmin and Replmon to troubleshoot any further problems.

Forcing Replication

1. For odd# computers, ensure that you are logged on as the default administrator of the domain*xx* domain. For even# computers, ensure that you are logged on as the default administrator of the child*xx* domain.

2. Open the Active Directory Sites And Services console. Click Start, click Administrative Tools, and then click Active Directory Sites And Services. In the left window pane, expand the Sites folder, and then expand the Default-First-Site-Name.

3. Expand the Servers folder and then expand the computer name of the computer you are logged on.

4. In the left console pane, click NTDS Settings.

5. In the right details pane, click the connection that you want to use to force replication. There should be only one connection currently.

6. Right-click the connection, and then click Replicate Now. A Replicate Now message box appears, as shown in the following graphic. The message should indicate that Active Directory has replicated the connections. Click OK.

   NOTE The Replicate Now dialog box might display the following error message: "The following error occurred during the attempt to synchronize naming context Configuration from domain controller COMPUTERxx to domain controller COMPUTERyy: The naming context is in the process of being removed or is not replicated from the specified server. The operation will not continue." If this error message displays, wait a few minutes for the domain controllers to synchronize and then try again to force a replication.

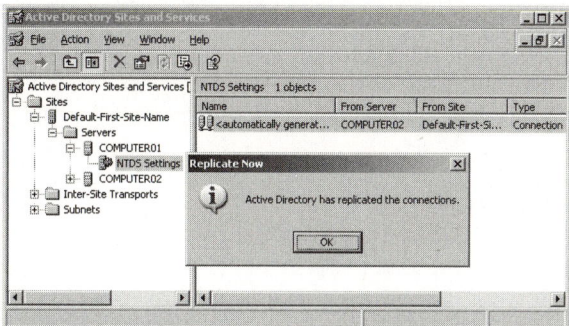

7. Close the Active Directory Sites And Services console.

Managing Connection Objects

Suppose your attempt to force replication didn't work. In this case, you could check the Event Viewer's Directory Service log to learn what occurred. You decide there may be a problem with the connection objects and decide to create one manually.

1. Open the Active Directory Sites And Services console. In the left console pane, expand the Sites folder, and then expand the Default-First-Site-Name.

2. Expand the Servers folder and then expand the computer name of the computer you are logged on to.

3. In the left console pane, click NTDS Settings.

4. Right-click NTDS Settings, and then click New Active Directory Connection. The Find Domain Controllers dialog box appears.

5. Select the computer name of the opposite computer. For example, if you are on Computer01, select Computer02 from the list of computer names displayed in the search results window pane. Click OK. An Active Directory message box appears.

6. A message appears indicating that there already is a connection and asks you if you want to create another connection. Click Yes. A New Object—Connection dialog box appears. Use the default settings, and then click OK. The new connection is created.

7. Force replication on the new connection object as described in the previous section.

   QUESTION *How can you tell which connections are the automatically generated connections and which connections are manually created connections?*

   Assume that you checked the Event Viewer and the same problem exists, so the connection object you just created can be deleted.

8. In the right details pane, click the connection that you want to delete. There should be two connections: the automatically generated connection and the manually created connection. Select the manually created connection. Right-click the connection and click Delete. An Active Directory message box appears.

9. Click Yes to confirm that you want to delete the connection object. The object is deleted.

Identifying the Global Catalog

While performing your replication checks, you learn that certain users are unable to log on to the network. You begin to wonder if the global catalog server is functional. You need to check to see which server is functioning as the global catalog server.

1. In the Active Directory Sites and Services console's left window pane, right-click NTDS Settings, and click Properties. The NTDS Settings Properties dialog box appears. On the General tab, you can see the Global Catalog check box. Click Cancel.

   QUESTION *What does it mean when the Global Catalog check box is selected?*

2. Close the Active Directory Sites And Services console.

Installing Windows Support Tools

You discover that the user logon issues were related to unplugged network adapters. Now you are anxious to continue troubleshooting the replication issues. You decide to work with some of the Windows Support Tools utilities to troubleshoot replication issues. If you haven't done so already, install the Windows Support Tools on your computer.

1. Insert the Microsoft Windows Server 2003 Evaluation CD-ROM into your computer.

2. Exit the startup screen if it appears and open the Support\Tools folder on the CD-ROM.

3. Double-click the file named Suptools.MSI. The Windows Support Tools Setup Wizard appears. Click Next.

4. Read the End User License Agreement and accept the licensing terms. Click Next.

5. Using the default settings, follow the remaining steps in the wizard to install the Windows Support Tools.

Using Repadmin

You decide to force replication with Repadmin this time. You also want to verify your replication partner connections.

1. Open a command prompt window.

2. On the odd# computer, in the command prompt window, type **repadmin /syncall domain.*xx*.local**. On the even# computer, type **repadmin /syncall child.*xx*.domain.*xx*.local**.

3. Read all of the CALLBACK MESSAGE. Confirm that there is a CALLBACK MESSAGE, which states: The Following Replication Completed Successfully. All domain controllers are now synchronized.

4. On the odd# computer, type **repadmin /showrepl domain.*xx*.local**. On the even# computer, type **repadmin /showrepl child.*xx*.domain.*xx*.local**.

    QUESTION Who are your inbound neighbors?

5. Type **cls** and press ENTER to clear the screen.

6. On the odd# computer, type **repadmin /showconn domain.*xx*.local**. On the even# computer type **repadmin /showconn child.*xx*.domain.*xx*.local**.

    QUESTION How many connections were found?

7. Close the command prompt window.

Using Replication Monitor

Now that you've successfully forced replication, you decide to use Replication Monitor to view your replication topology. Use the Active Directory Replication Monitor to check the replication topology.

> **NOTE** To perform this lab you must be logged on as a member of the Enterprise Admins group. For odd# computers, you should be logged on as the default administrator of the domain*xx* domain. For even# computers, you should be logged on as the default administrator of the domain*xx* domain, not the child*xx* domain.

1. On even# computers, log on as the default administrator of the domain*xx* domain. (On odd# computers, you should already be logged on as default administrator of the domain*xx* domain.)

2. Run the Active Directory Replication Monitor. Click Start, click Run, and type **replmon.exe**. Click OK. Active Directory Replication Monitor appears.

3. Expand the Active Directory Replication Monitor if necessary. The left console pane shows information for monitored servers. Currently there should not be any servers listed.

4. Right-click Monitored Servers, and then click Add Monitored Server. The Add Server To Monitor dialog box appears.

5. Select the Search The Directory For Server To Add option button. In the text box where you enter the name of a domain in the forest from which to read site data, there is an automatic entry made. Click Next, and the next screen appears.

6. Expand the Default-First-Site-Name, and select a server to monitor. Choose the odd# computer, and click Finish.

7. Add the even# computer into the Active Directory Replication Monitor. Right-click Monitored Servers, and then click Add Monitored Server. The Add Server To Monitor dialog box appears.

8. Verify the Add The Server Explicitly By Name option button is selected, and then click Next.

9. Type the even# computer name in the text box below the statement Enter The Name Of The Server To Monitor Explicitly, and then click Finish.

10. Take a screen capture of the Active Directory Replication Monitor window with both computer objects expanded. Resize the window if necessary so that you can read both computer names as well as the names of their subordinate objects. Save the screen capture as a bitmap named Ex3-1 on the C: drive of your computer.

11. In the Active Directory Replication Monitor, right-click the object representing of the computer you are using, and then click Show Replication Topologies. The View Replication Topology dialog box opens.

12. At the top of the dialog box click View, and then click Connection Objects Only. In the center of the dialog box, the connection objects appear.

13. Right-click either computer object, and then click Show Intra-Site Connections. A line is drawn between connection objects that have a connection, as shown in the following graphic.

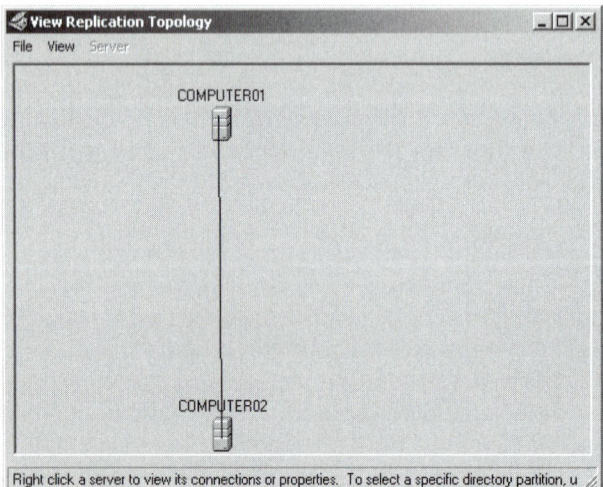

14. Close the View Replication Topology dialog box.
15. Close the Active Directory Replication Monitor.

EXERCISE 3-2: PREPARING YOUR INFRASTRUCTURE

Estimated completion time: 5 minutes

You want to configure your existing network to support a new site. You can run some tests to see how a custom application will perform. However, you are unable to locate a router or additional network cards. You decide that you can create a logical Internet Protocol (IP) network inside your physical local area network (LAN) for your tests. You need to prepare two servers for this test.

WARNING *Some of the steps in this exercise should be performed on only one computer in each pair. You will be informed which computer (odd# or even#) to use in the first step of each portion of this exercise.*

Preparing odd# Computers for Sites

1. On the odd# computer, open the Local Area Connection Properties dialog box. Click Start, click Control Panel, and then click Network Connections. Right-click Local Area Connection, and then click Properties. A Local Area Connection Properties dialog box opens.

2. Select Internet Protocol (TCP/IP), and then click Properties. The Internet Protocol (TCP/IP) Properties dialog box opens.

3. Click Advanced. The Advanced TCP/IP Settings dialog box appears.

4. In the IP Addresses box, click Add. The TCP/IP Address dialog box opens.

5. Type the IP address **192.168.*x*.*x*** for the IP address and type **255.255.255.0** for the subnet mask, and click Add. The example settings for Computer05 are shown in the following figure.

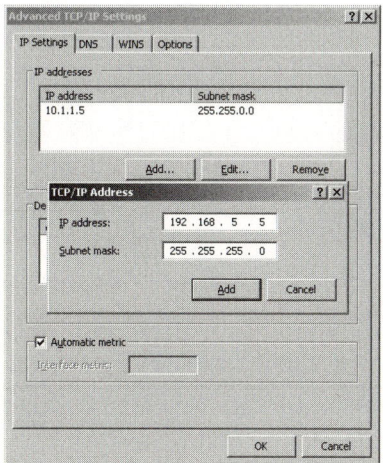

6. Click OK in the Advanced TCP/IP Settings dialog box.
7. Click OK in the Internet Protocol (TCP/IP) Properties dialog box.
8. Click Close in the Local Area Connection Properties dialog box.

Preparing even# Computers for Sites

1. On the even# computer, open the Local Area Connection Properties dialog box.
2. Select Internet Protocol (TCP/IP), and then click Properties. The Internet Protocol (TCP/IP) Properties dialog box opens.
3. Take a screen capture of the Internet Protocol (TCP/IP) Properties window. Save this screen capture as a bitmap named Ex3-2 on your C: drive.
4. In the Use The Following IP Address box, type the IP address **192.168.*x.y*** for the IP address and type **255.255.255.0** for the subnet mask.
5. Clear the Default Gateway box if there is an address in the box.
6. Set the Preferred DNS server to **192.168.*x.x***.

The example settings for Computer06 are shown in the following figure.

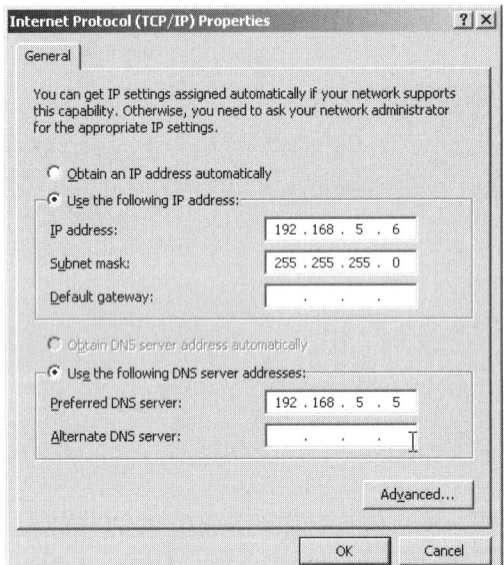

7. Clear the Alternate DNS Server box if there is an address in the box, and then click OK.
8. Click Close in the Local Area Connection Properties dialog box.

Restarting odd# and even# Computers

1. Once the site changes have been made, shut down both the odd# and even# computers.
2. Restart the odd# computer, keeping the even# computer shut down.
3. On the odd# computer, log on as the default administrator of the domain*xx* domain.
4. Restart the even# computer.
5. On the even# computer, log on as the default administrator of the domain*xx* domain.

EXERCISE 3-3: CONFIGURING A SITE

Estimated completion time: 5 minutes

You decide to create two sites: Main and Branch. Furthermore, you want to rename the Default-First-Site-Name to HQ.

Creating a Site for odd# Computers

1. On the odd# computer, open the Active Directory Sites And Services console.
2. In the left console pane, right-click Sites, and then click New Site. The New Object—Site dialog box appears.
3. In the Name text box, type **MainSite**. Click DEFAULTIPSITELINK, and then click OK. A message box appears indicating that you must complete additional steps to configure the site, click OK.

Creating a Site for even# Computers and Renaming the Default-First-Site-Name

1. On the even# computer, open the Active Directory Sites And Services console.

    NOTE *If an error is displayed when you open Active Directory Sites And Services that indicates that naming information cannot be located, wait a few minutes to ensure the two domain controllers have had time to replicate and try opening the console again.*

2. In the left console pane, right-click Sites, and then click New Site. The New Object—Site dialog box appears.
3. In the Name text box, type **BranchSite**. Click DEFAULTIPSITELINK, and then click OK. A message box appears indicating that you must complete additional steps to configure the site, click OK.

4. In the left console pane of the Active Directory Sites And Services console, right-click the Default-First-Site-Name, and then click Rename. Type **HQ** as the new name for Default-First-Site-Name, and press Enter.

EXERCISE 3-4: CONFIGURING A NEW SUBNET

Estimated completion time: 5 minutes

You decide to create two subnets for your new sites.

Even# Computer Subnet Creation

1. On the even# computer, open the Active Directory Sites And Services console. Right-click Subnets, and then click New Subnet. The New Object—Subnet dialog box appears.

2. Type **192.168.*x*.0** in the Address text box and type **255.255.255.0** in the Mask text box. Click BranchSite, and then click OK. The following graphic is an example of Computer06.

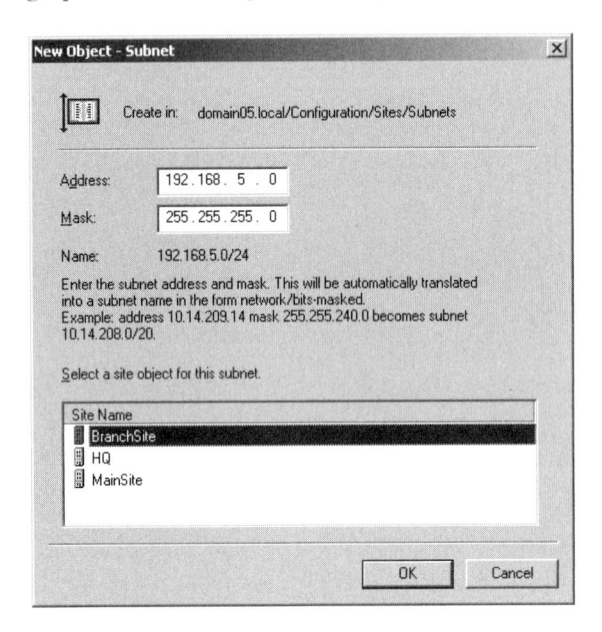

Odd# Computer Subnet Creation

1. On the odd# computer, in the left console pane of the Active Directory Sites And Services console, right-click Subnets, and then click New Subnet. The New Object—Subnet dialog box appears.

2. Type **10.1.0.0** in the Address text box and type **255.255.0.0** in the Mask text box, as shown in the following graphic. Click MainSite, and then click OK.

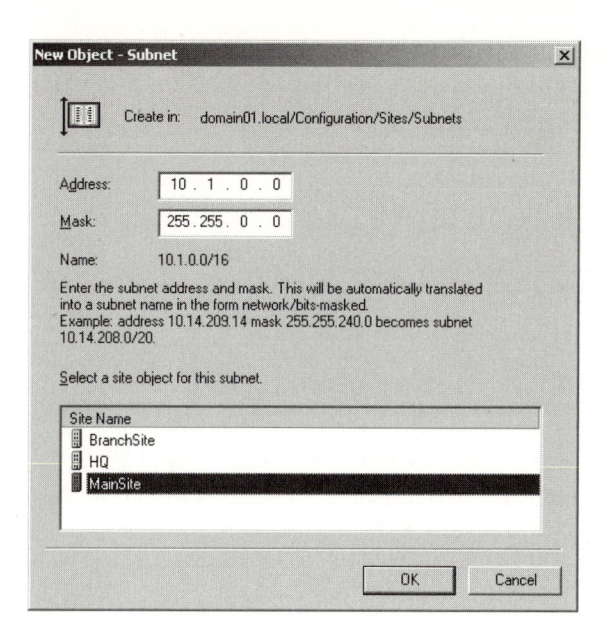

EXERCISE 3-5: MOVING COMPUTERS AND CREATING SITE LINKS

Estimated completion time: 15 minutes

Now that you have sites and subnets, you want to move your computer accounts into their respective sites and configure site links.

Moving the odd# and even# Computer to the Appropriate Site

1. On the odd# computer, open Active Directory Sites And Services. Ensure that the Default-First-Site-Name was renamed to HQ. If you don't see this on the odd# computer, force replication, and refresh the view. If a replication error is displayed, wait a few moments and test again.

2. In the left console pane of Active Directory Sites And Services console, expand HQ, and then expand Servers.

3. Right-click Computer*xx*, and then click Move. The Move Server dialog box appears.

4. Click MainSite, and then click OK.

5. In the left window pane, expand MainSite and then expand the Servers object below MainSite. You should see the odd# computer object.

6. Try to force replication using the connection object of the odd# computer. You should see a message indicating that these servers are in different sites. Click OK. You need a site link to allow replication between these two domain controllers. The following graphic is an example for Computer01.

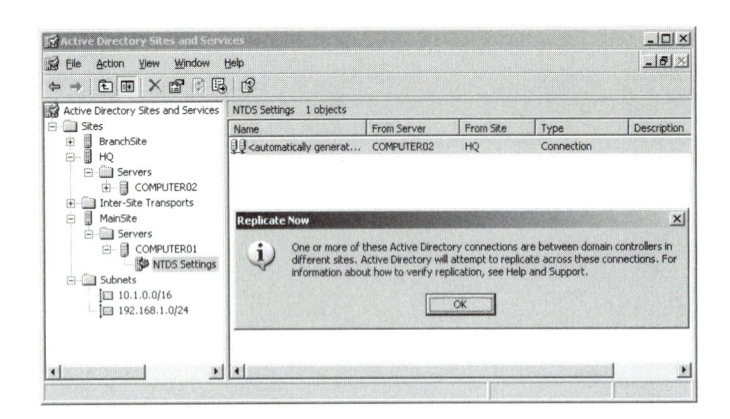

7. Right-click Computer*yy*, and then click Move. The Move Server dialog box appears.

8. Click BranchSite, and then click OK.

9. In the left window pane, expand BranchSite and then the Servers object. You should see the even# computer object.

10. Try to force replication using the connection object of the even# computer. You should see a message indicating that these servers are in different sites. Click OK. You need a site link to allow replication between these two domain controllers.

Creating a Site Link from the even# Computer

1. On the even# computer, in the left console pane of the Active Directory Sites And Services console, expand Inter-Site Transports. Right-click IP, and click New Site Link. The New Object—Site Link dialog box appears.

2. In the Name text box, type **EvenLink**. In the Sites Not In This Site Link box, click MainSite, and then click Add.

3. In the Sites Not In This Site Link box, click BranchSite, and then click Add. Click OK.

4. Click the IP object under Inter-Site Transports. The EvenLink should be visible in the right window pane.

5. Right-click the EvenLink and click Properties. The EvenLink Properties dialog box opens.

6. Change the Replicate Every box to read **15** Minutes. Click OK.

Creating a Site Link from the odd# Computer

1. On the odd# computer, in the left console pane of the Active Directory Sites And Services console, expand Inter-Site Transports. Right-click IP, and click New Site Link. The New Object—Site Link dialog box appears.

2. In the Name text box, type **OddLink**. In the Sites Not In This Site Link box, click MainSite, and then click Add.

3. In the Sites Not In This Site Link box, click BranchSite, and then click Add. Click OK.

   NOTE *In a production environment, you would typically create a single Site Link to link two sites.*

4. Click the IP object under Inter-Site Transports. The OddLink should be visible in the right window pane.

5. Right-click the OddLink and click Properties. The OddLink Properties dialog box opens.

6. Change the Replicate Every box to read **15** Minutes. Click OK.

Verifying Replication

1. Complete the Lab Review Questions. In 15 minutes or more return to the odd# or even# computer. Refresh the Active Directory Sites and Services console by pressing the F5 key or clicking the Refresh button on the toolbar. You should see the opposite link (OddLink or EvenLink) added as a Site Link as shown in the following figure. This is verification that your computers are replicating with each other.

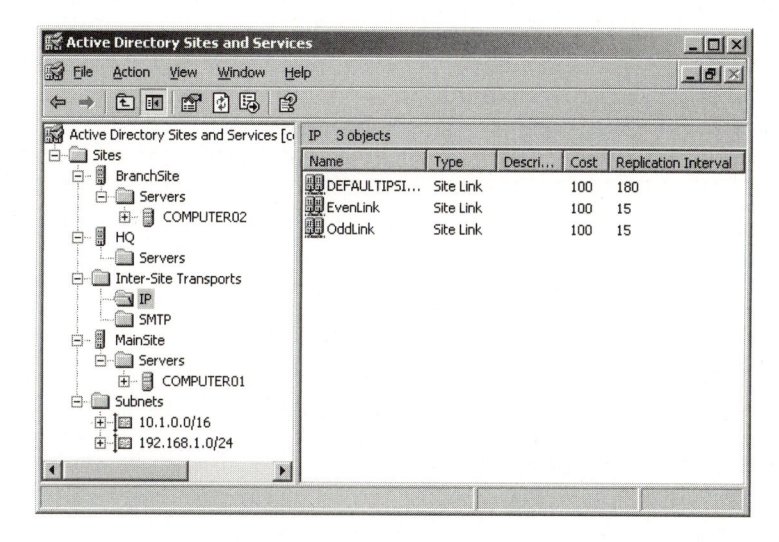

2. Complete the Lab Challenges. If you do not complete the Lab Challenges, you must perform the Lab Cleanup before you can move on to Lab 4.

LAB REVIEW QUESTIONS

Estimated completion time: 15 minutes

1. In your words, describe what you learned during this lab.
2. Which default administrative group has the privileges necessary to create and monitor sites?

3. In a multi-domain environment, what is the main difference between the partitions on a domain controller that is also a global catalog server versus other domain controllers that are not global catalog servers?

4. Which utility allows you to view a graphical representation of intersite connections?

5. What major tasks are required to create an Active Directory site?

LAB CHALLENGE 3-1: CONFIGURING PREFERRED BRIDGEHEAD SERVER FOR SITES

Estimated completion time: 10 minutes

You noticed that the knowledge consistency checker (KCC) isn't selecting the server you want Active Directory to use as the bridgehead server in each site. You decide to configure a preferred bridgehead server for your site.

Configure the odd# computer as the preferred bridgehead server for the MainSite. Configure the even# computer as the preferred bridgehead server for the BranchSite.

LAB CHALLENGE 3-2: MAKING THE EVEN# COMPUTER A GLOBAL CATALOG SERVER

Estimated completion time: 20 minutes

You decide to make the computer in the BranchSite a global catalog server.

Configure the even# server as a global catalog server.

> **QUESTION** Use the technique you learned in Exercise 3-1: Replication Management under the heading Using Replication Monitor to view the naming contexts of the even# computer. Compare the screen capture of Active Directory Replication Monitor you took in Exercise 3-1 to what you see here and explain the differences. You may need to wait 15 minutes for replication to occur before you notice any difference. You also have the option of using the Replication Monitor to force replication to occur. See if you can find that option.

POST-LAB CLEANUP

Estimated completion time: 10 minutes

Use the techniques you learned in this lab to complete the following steps from either computer (but not both):

1. Ensure you are logged on as the default administrator of the domain*xx* domain.

2. Move the odd# computer object and the even# computer object to the HQ site.

3. Rename the HQ site to Default-First-Site-Name.

4. Clear the Global Catalog check box on the even# computer's NTDS Settings Properties dialog box.

5. Delete the two sites you created in this lab. To delete a site in the Active Directory Sites And Services console, right-click the site object you want to delete and then click Delete. Confirm this action by clicking Yes on the two warning message boxes that appear (one after the other).

6. Delete the two subnets you created in this lab. To delete a subnet in the Active Directory Sites And Services console, expand the Subnets object, right-click the subnet object that you want to delete and click Delete. Confirm this action by clicking Yes on the warning message that appears.

7. Delete the two site links that you created in this lab. To delete a site link in the Active Directory Sites And Service console, expand the Inter-Site Transports object and then select the IP object. In the right window pane, right-click the Site Link object that you would like to delete and click Delete. Confirm this action by clicking Yes on the warning message that appears.

8. Reset the TCP/IP configuration of the even# computer. Reference the screen capture you took named Ex3-2 on your C: drive.

9. Remove the additional IP address configured for the odd# server.

10. Restart the odd# computer.

11. Once the odd# computer has finished restarting, restart the even# computer.

LAB 4
GLOBAL CATALOG AND FLEXIBLE SINGLE MASTER OPERATIONS (FSMO) ROLES

This lab contains the following exercises and activities:

- Exercise 4-1: Global Catalog and the Mixed Functional Level Domain
- Exercise 4-2: Global Catalog and the Native Functional Level Domain
- Exercise 4-3: Enabling Universal Group Membership Caching
- Exercise 4-4: Working with Flexible Single Master Operations Roles
- Lab Review Questions
- Lab Challenge 4-1: Using the DNS Console to Verify Global Catalog Records on the DNS Server
- Lab Challenge 4-2: Verifying FSMO Role Holders with Dcdiag
- Lab Challenge 4-3: Determining Whether an Attribute is Replicated in the Global Catalog

You are a network administrator for the Baldwin Museum of Science. The Active Directory configuration of your company consists of two domains. These domains are configured in a parent-child relationship. Both of these domains are using the Microsoft Windows 2000 mixed functional level. The forest is in Windows 2000 functional level. The first domain controller in your domain is the only global catalog server and holds all of the Flexible Single Master Operations (FSMO) roles.

There are five domain controllers on your network. All of your domain controllers run Microsoft Windows Server 2003, Enterprise Edition. Three domain controllers are in the parent domain and two are in the child domain. There are also 500 client computers running Microsoft Windows XP Professional. Another 200 client computers are running Microsoft Windows 2000 Professional.

Several members of the management team want to have groups that can be used forest-wide. They are considering changing the domain functional levels to Windows 2000 native in order to create universal groups. Your manager has attended a few of these discussions and she is concerned that the global catalog server could be a single point of failure for your company. She doesn't want users to be unable to log on if the global catalog server is not online. She has asked you to help run some tests to explore the implications of moving to Windows 2000 native functional level.

After completing this lab, you will be able to:

- Convert a domain from Windows 2000 mixed to Windows 2000 native functional level.
- Diagnose logon failures related to global catalog server outages.
- Enable universal group membership caching.
- Determine FSMO role holders using Ntdsutil and Dcdiag.
- Verify global catalog records are registered on the Domain Name System (DNS) server.
- Determine whether an attribute is replicated in the global catalog.

Estimated lesson time: 160 minutes

> **NOTE** In this lab you will see the characters **xx**, **yy**, and **zz**. These directions assume that you are working on computers configured in pairs and that each computer has a number. One number is odd and the other number is even For example, Computer01 is the odd# computer and Computer02 is the even# computer. When you see **xx**, substitute the unique number assigned to the odd# computer. When you see **yy**, substitute the unique number assigned to the even# computer. When you see **zz**, substitute the number assigned to the computer you are working at, either odd or even.
>
> Whenever you see the Manage Your Server page appear in this lab, select the Don't Display This Page At Logon check box and close the Manage Your Server page.

LAB DEPENDENCIES

- The even# computer must be configured to use the odd# computer as its Preferred DNS Server, as explained in Exercise 1-4.
- Active Directory is installed on the odd# computer. Lab 2, Exercise 2-1 covers the installation of Active Directory on the odd# computer.
- Active Directory is installed on the even# computer. Lab 2, Exercise 2-3 and 2-4 cover the installation of Active Directory on the even# computer.
- Support Tools must be installed, as described in Lab 3, Exercise 3.1.

EXERCISE 4-1: GLOBAL CATALOG AND THE MIXED FUNCTIONAL LEVEL DOMAIN

Estimated completion time: 30 minutes

Although your domain functional level is Windows 2000 mixed, your manager is concerned that a failure of the server that hosts the global catalog could prevent network users from logging on. You need to conduct some trials to ensure that a global catalog failure will not prevent users from logging on.

Verifying the Global Catalog is Operational

First, you want to ensure that your global catalog is listening on the correct Transmission Control Protocol (TCP) port.

1. On the odd# computer, log on as the default administrator of the domain*xx* domain. On the even# computer, log on as the default administrator of the child*xx* domain.
2. Open a command prompt window.
3. Type **netstat -a -n**, and press ENTER.
4. Look at the results to see if port TCP 3268 appears in the list by looking for an entry that shows TCP 0.0.0.0:3268.

    QUESTION *If port 3268 is listed, what does this mean? If not, what does it mean?*

5. Close the command prompt window.

Verifying Functional Levels

1. On the odd# computer, open the Active Directory Domains And Trusts console.

    NOTE *To open the Active Directory Domains And Trusts console, click Start, click Administrative Tools, and then click Active Directory Domains And Trusts. Alternatively, you can open the Run dialog box, type* **domain.msc**, *and then click OK.*

2. Right-click Active Directory Domains And Trusts in the left console pane, and then click Raise Forest Functional Level. The Raise Forest Functional Level dialog box appears.
3. Read the displayed message.
4. Click OK.

    QUESTION *The dialog box contains a list of reasons describing why you cannot raise the forest functional level. Based on the current configuration of the lab computers, what is the reason the forest functional level cannot be raised?*

5. Right-click the object that represents your domain, domain*xx*.local, and click Raise Domain Functional Level.
6. Verify that your domain functional level is currently Windows 2000 mixed.
7. Click Cancel. You do *not* want to raise the functional level. You'll need Windows 2000 mixed domain functional level for the following experiment to work properly.
8. Close the Active Directory Domains And Trusts console.

Adding Experimental User Accounts to the Parent Domain

1. On the odd# computer, open the Active Directory Users And Computers console.

   NOTE To open the Active Directory Users And Computers console, click Administrative Tools, and then click Active Directory Users And Computers. Alternatively, you can open the Run dialog box, type **dsa.msc**, and then click OK.

2. Expand the parent domain object, domain*xx*.local, in the left console pane.

3. Right-click the Users folder, click New, and then click User. The New Object - User dialog box appears.

4. Create a new user account named User*xx* in the default Users container. Click the Full Name text box, and enter **User*xx***.

5. Click the User Logon Name text box, type the same name used in step 4 into this text box, and then click Next, as shown in the following example for Computer01.

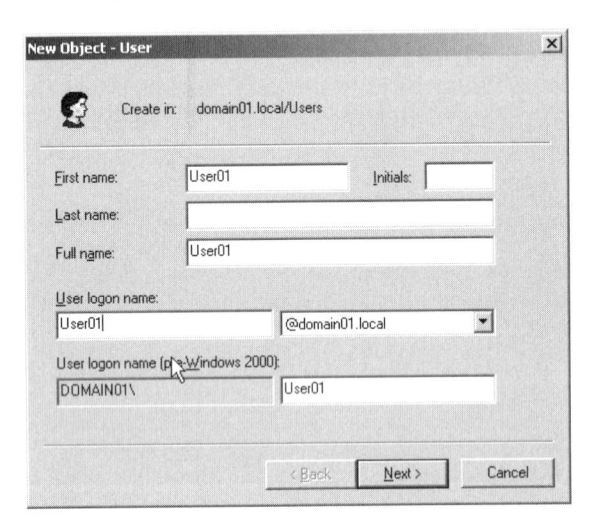

6. Type **MSPress#1** into the Password text box and Confirm Password text box.

7. Clear the User Must Change Password At Next Logon check box. Click Next, and then click Finish.

8. Create a new user account named User*yy* in the default Users container for your domain. Repeat steps 3 through 7 to add User*yy*.

9. Close the Active Directory Users and Computers console.

Adding Experimental User Accounts to the Child Domain

1. On the even# computer, open the Active Directory Users And Computers console.

   NOTE To open the Active Directory Users And Computers console, click Administrative Tools, and then click Active Directory Users And Computers. Alternatively, you can open the Run dialog box, type **dsa.msc**, and then click OK.

2. Expand the child domain object, child*xx*.domain*xx*.local, in the left console pane.

3. Right-click the Users folder, click New, and then click User. The New Object - User dialog box appears.

4. Click the Full Name text box, and enter **Childuser*xx***.

5. Click the User Logon Name text box, type the same name used in step 4 into this text box, and then click Next, as shown in the following example for Computer02.

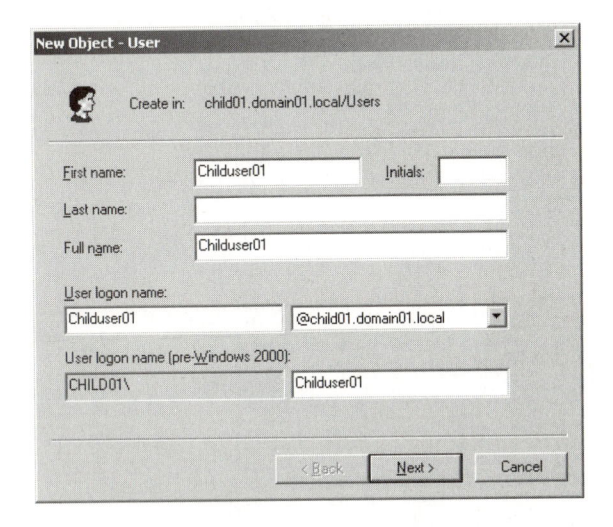

6. Type **MSPress#1** in the Password text box and Confirm Password text box.

7. Clear the User Must Change Password At Next Logon check box. Click Next, and then Finish.

8. Repeat steps 3 through 7 to add Childuser*yy*.

9. Close the Active Directory Users and Computers console.

Allowing Users to Log On to Domain Controllers

CAUTION You are about to allow users to log on to a domain controller. You are doing this only for testing purposes. You typically would not want domain users to be able to interactively (locally) log on to a domain controller.

1. On both the odd# and even# computers, open the Default Domain Controller Security Settings console.

    NOTE To open the Default Domain Controller Security Settings console, click Start, click Administrative Tools, and then click Domain Controller Security Policy.

2. In the left console pane, expand Local Policies, and then click User Rights Assignment. Policy objects appear in the right window pane.

3. In the right window pane, double-click the Allow Logon Locally policy object. The Allow Logon Locally Properties dialog box appears, as shown in the following figure.

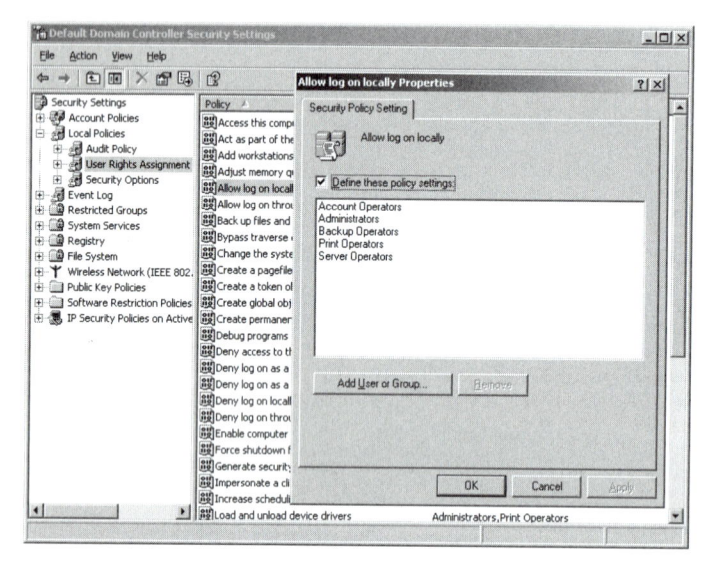

4. Click Add User Or Group. An Add User Or Group dialog box appears.

5. Type **Users** in the User And Group Names text box, click OK, and then click OK again in the Allow Logon Locally Properties dialog box.

6. Close the Default Domain Controller Security Settings console.

Simulating a Global Catalog Failure

1. On the odd# computer, open the Active Directory Sites And Services console.

2. Expand Sites, Default-First-Site-Name, Servers, and then click computer*xx*.

3. In the right window pane, right-click NTDS Settings, and then click Properties.

4. Clear the Global Catalog check box, and then click OK.

5. Close Active Directory Sites And Services.

Logging On Using UPNs for User Accounts

NOTE A User Principal Name (UPN) is as follows: username@domainname, for example, Childuser01@child01.domain01.local or User01@domain01.local.

1. On the odd# computer, log off the Administrator. Log on using the UPN for User*xx*.

2. On the even# computer, log off the Administrator. Log on using the UPN for Childuser*xx*.

    NOTE If you see a message that reads "The local policy of this system does not permit you to logon interactively," wait a few minutes and try again.

    QUESTION Did you require a global catalog server in order to log on? Why?

3. Log off both the computers.

EXERCISE 4-2: GLOBAL CATALOG AND THE NATIVE FUNCTIONAL LEVEL DOMAIN

Estimated completion time: 30 minutes

Your manager wants to know what would happen if you raised your domain functional level to Windows 2000 native and the global catalog server failed. She has asked you to run some tests on your test network to see what differences there are between user logons in a mixed versus native functional level domain. She specifically wants to know if there is a greater dependency on the global catalog server.

Raising Parent Domain Functional Level

1. On the odd# computer, log on as the default administrator of domain*xx* domain.

2. Open the Active Directory Domains And Trusts console.

3. Right-click the object that represents the parent domain, and then click Raise Domain Functional Level. The Raise Domain Functional Level dialog box appears.

4. In the drop-down selection box, ensure Windows 2000 native appears, and click Raise. A message box appears.

5. Read the message, and confirm by clicking OK. When another message box appears confirming that the domain functional level has been raised, click OK.

6. Close the Active Directory Domains And Trusts console.

7. Log off the computer.

Raising Child Domain Functional Level

1. On the even# computer, log on as the default administrator of child*xx* domain.
2. Open the Active Directory Domains And Trusts console.
3. Expand the parent domain to display the child domain.
4. Right-click the object that represents the child domain, and then click Raise Domain Functional Level. The Raise Domain Functional Level dialog box appears.
5. In the drop-down selection box, ensure that Windows 2000 native appears, and then click Raise. A message box appears.
6. Read the message, and confirm by clicking OK. When another message box appears confirming that the domain functional level has been raised, click OK.
7. Close the Active Directory Domains And Trusts console.
8. Log off the computer.

Discovering a Logon Issue

1. On the odd# computer, attempt to log on using the UPN for User*xx*.
2. On the even# computer, attempt to log on using the UPN for Childuser*xx*.

    QUESTION When you try to log on, what is the result? Explain the issue.

Resolving the Global Catalog Outage

1. On the even# computer, log on as the default administrator of the domain*xx* domain. Note that the domain is domain*xx* and not the child*xx* domain.
2. Open the Active Directory Replication Monitor, and add the even# computer for monitoring. See Lab Exercise 3-1 if you need help using Replmon.
3. Right-click the object that represents the even# computer, and click Show Global Catalog Servers In Enterprise. Read the message, and click OK.

    QUESTION What did you learn about your enterprise network?

    NOTE If you see a dialog box that indicates the odd# computer was the global catalog server, wait a few minutes for replication to occur and try again.

4. Enable the global catalog. Open the Active Directory Sites And Services console. Expand Sites, Default-First-Site-Name, and then Servers. Click Computer*xx*. In the right window pane, right-click NTDS Settings, and then click Properties. Select the Global Catalog check box, and then click OK.

5. Switch to Active Directory Replication Monitor, and try the Show Global Catalog Servers In Enterprise option again. This time the Show Global Catalog Servers dialog box opens displaying the odd# computer as a Global Catalog server. Click OK.

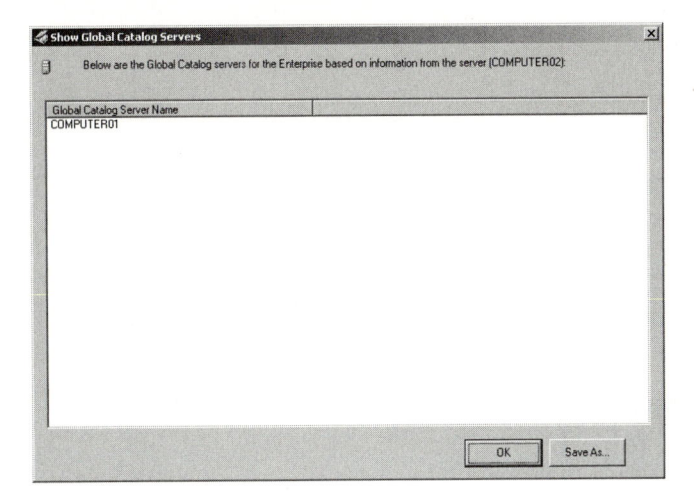

6. Close all open windows.

7. Log off the computer.

Logging On to the Child Domain

NOTE Wait at least five minutes after performing the previous activity before you perform the following procedure.

1. On the odd# computer, attempt to log on to the parent domain using the UPN for User*xx*.

2. On the even# computer, attempt to log on to the child domain using the UPN for Childuser*xx*.

3. Log off both computers.

QUESTION Why were your logon attempts successful this time?

EXERCISE 4-3: ENABLING UNIVERSAL GROUP MEMBERSHIP CACHING

Estimated completion time: 25 minutes

Your manager is now curious whether the new universal group membership caching feature will alleviate her concerns about user logon dependency on the global catalog. You decide to run an experiment in your test lab to see how universal group membership caching works in the event of a global catalog failure.

Enabling Universal Group Membership Caching

1. On the odd# computer, log on as the default administrator of the domain*xx* domain.

2. Open the Active Directory Sites And Services console.

3. In the left console pane, expand Sites, and then expand Default-First-Site-Name if necessary.

4. Click Default-First-Name-Site.

5. In the right window pane, right-click NTDS Settings, and then click Properties. An NTDS Site Settings Properties dialog box appears.

6. Select the Enable Universal Membership Group Caching check box, and then click OK.

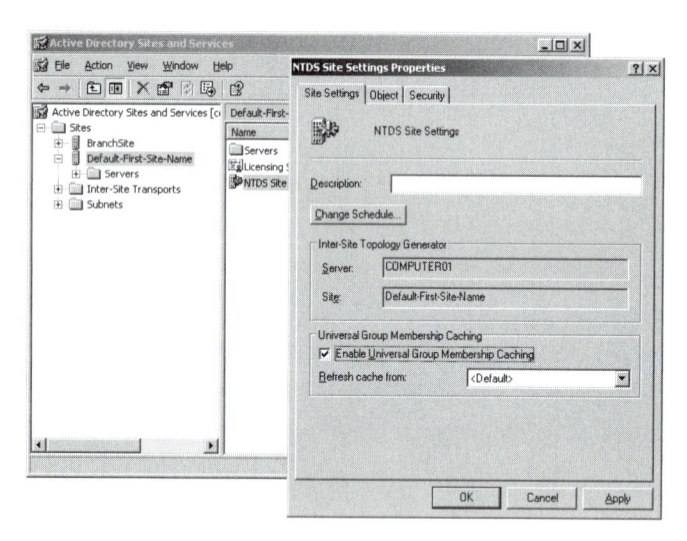

7. Force Active Directory replication using any one of the techniques you learned in previous labs.

Logging On With Universal Group Membership Caching Enabled

1. On the even# computer, log on to the child domain using the UPN for Childuser*yy*. Note that the domain is Childuser*yy* and not the Childuser*xx* domain.

2. Log off the even# computer.

Simulating a Global Catalog Failure

1. On the odd# computer, in Active Directory Sites And Services, clear the Global Catalog check box in the NTDS Settings Properties dialog box of the odd# computer and click OK. See Exercise 4-1 for detailed steps if you need them. This simulates a global catalog server failure.

Testing User Logon Without the Global Catalog

1. On the even# computer, log on to the child domain using the UPN for Childuser*yy*.

   QUESTION *Why did this logon succeed, even though the global catalog server is not available?*

2. Log off the even# computer.

3. On the even# computer, attempt to log on to the child domain using the UPN for Childuser*xx*.

   QUESTION *Why does this logon attempt fail?*

4. Ensure that you are logged off the even# computer.

5. Configure the odd# computer as a global catalog server.

6. Disable universal group membership caching for the Default-First-Site-Name site.

EXERCISE 4-4: WORKING WITH FLEXIBLE SINGLE MASTER OPERATIONS ROLES

Estimated completion time: 15 minutes

Your manager tells you that the computer holding the schema operations master role must be replaced soon. She asks you to transfer that role to another server for a short period while a new server can be put in place.

Viewing Operations Masters

First you must determine which server holds the schema operations master role.

1. On the even# computer, log on as the default administrator of the domain*xx* domain.
2. Open the Run dialog box and type **ntdsutil**, and then press ENTER.
3. Type **domain management**, and then press ENTER.
4. Type **connections**, and then press ENTER.
5. Type **connect to server computer*xx*** and then press ENTER.
6. Type **quit**, and then press ENTER.
7. Type **select operation target**, and then press ENTER.
8. Type **list roles for connected server**, and then press ENTER. Review the outputs.

   QUESTION *What FSMO roles are assigned to the odd# computer?*

9. Type **quit**.
10. Type **connections**, and then press ENTER.
11. Type **connect to server *computeryy*** and press ENTER.
12. Type **quit**, and then press ENTER.
13. Type **select operation target**, and then press ENTER.
14. Type **list roles for connected server**, and then press ENTER. Review the output.

    QUESTION What FSMO roles are assigned to the even# computer?

15. Close the Ntdsutil window.

Transferring the Schema Master to a Different Domain Controller

Next you must move the schema operations master to another domain controller.

NOTE You should always leave the schema operations master role on a domain controller in the forest root domain. You are performing this activity to get the experience of transferring an operations master role with Ntdsutil.

1. On the odd# computer, log on as the default administrator of the domain*xx* domain.

   NOTE In order to complete this exercise, the user account you use must be a member of Schema Admins or have user rights that allow schema management. The default domain administrator of the parent domain has the appropriate rights.

2. Open the Run dialog box and type **ntdsutil**, and then press ENTER.
3. Type **roles**, and then press ENTER.
4. Type **connections**, and then press ENTER.
5. Type **connect to server *computeryy*** and then press ENTER.
6. Type **quit**, and then press ENTER.
7. Type **transfer schema master**, and then press ENTER. A Role Transfer Confirmation dialog message appears.
8. Read the message, and then click Yes.
9. Review the output in the Ntdsutil window to confirm that the even# computer is now listed as the schema operations master. Close all open windows.

Transferring the Schema Master to the New Server

Assume the new server was built and put in place of the old server. Now you must transfer the schema operations master role to the new server.

> **NOTE** In this activity, you will move the schema operations master role back to the odd# computer.

1. On the even# computer, log on as the default administrator of the domain*xx* domain.

    > **NOTE** In order to complete this exercise, the user account you use must be a member of Schema Admins or have user rights that allow schema management. The default domain administrator of the parent domain has the appropriate rights.

2. Open the Run dialog box and type **ntdsutil**, and then press ENTER.
3. Type **roles**, and then press ENTER.
4. Type **connections**, and then press ENTER.
5. Type **connect to server *computerxx*** and then press ENTER.
6. Type **quit**, and then press ENTER.
7. Type **transfer schema master**, and then press ENTER. A Role Transfer Confirmation dialog message appears.
8. Read the message, and click Yes.
9. Review the output to confirm that the odd# computer is now listed as the schema operations master. Close all open windows.

LAB REVIEW QUESTIONS

Estimated completion time: 15 minutes

1. In your own words, describe what you learned during this lab.
2. You are the network administrator for an Active Directory domain that has five domain controllers. The domain functional level is set to Windows 2000 mixed. Only one domain controller is configured as a global catalog server. If that global catalog server fails, will it prevent users from logging on to the network?
3. What software utilities or Active Directory consoles can you use to determine which servers are configured as a global catalog servers?
4. You are the network administrator for an Active Directory domain that has four domain controllers and three sites. The domain functional level is set to Windows 2000 native. Only one domain controller is configured as a global catalog server. What options do you have to improve logon speed and fault tolerance in your network?
5. How many FSMO roles would you find in an Active Directory forest that had one parent and two child domains?

LAB CHALLENGE 4-1: USING THE DNS CONSOLE TO VERIFY GLOBAL CATALOG RECORDS ON THE DNS SERVER

Estimated completion time: 10 minutes

Another administrator says he is having trouble resolving some issues with a global catalog server that he just removed from the network. He wants you to check on the global catalog servers that are registered with the DNS server. You decide to use the DNS console to check these records.

On the odd# computer use the DNS console to locate global catalog SRV resource records in the domain.

LAB CHALLENGE 4-2: VERIFYING FSMO ROLE HOLDERS WITH DCDIAG

Estimated completion time: 15 minutes

Your manager tells you that another administrator transferred various FSMO roles as an experiment. She asks you to verify which servers hold all of the FSMO roles. You want to use DCDiag to output the FSMO role holders to a file named FSMO.txt on the C drive.

Locate the domain controllers that hold the FSMO roles in the enterprise using DCDiag.

> **NOTE** Use the command dcdiag /? to help you figure out the proper syntax.

LAB CHALLENGE 4-3: DETERMINING WHETHER AN ATTRIBUTE IS REPLICATED IN THE GLOBAL CATALOG

Estimated completion time: 20 minutes

Your manager wants to know if the sIDHistory attribute is maintained in the global catalog server.

Use the Active Directory Schema snap-in and locate the properties of the sIDHistory attribute.

> **NOTE** To use the Active Directory Schema snap-in, you must first register it. Search in the Help And Support Center in the Start menu on schmmgmt.msc for more information.

TROUBLESHOOTING LAB A

Troubleshooting Lab A is a practical application of the knowledge you have acquired from Labs 1 through 4. Troubleshooting Lab A is divided into two sections, "Reviewing a Network" and "Troubleshooting a Break Scenario." In the "Reviewing a Network" section, you will review and assess a Windows Server 2003 Active Directory infrastructure for City Power & Light. In the "Troubleshooting a Break Scenario," section, you will troubleshoot a particular break scenario. Your instructor or lab assistant has changed your computer configuration, causing it to "break." Your task in this section will be to apply your acquired skills to troubleshoot and resolve the break.

REVIEWING A NETWORK

In this portion of Troubleshooting Lab A, you are the network administrator for City Power & Light (*http://www.cpandl.com*). City Power & Light has five different locations named Central, Northwest, Northeast, Southwest, and Southeast. The Central location has 500 client computers and two network servers. The Northwest and Northeast locations have approximately 75 client computers and one server computer each. The Southwest and Southeast locations have 100 client computers and one network server each. Figure A-1 illustrates the company's network infrastructure.

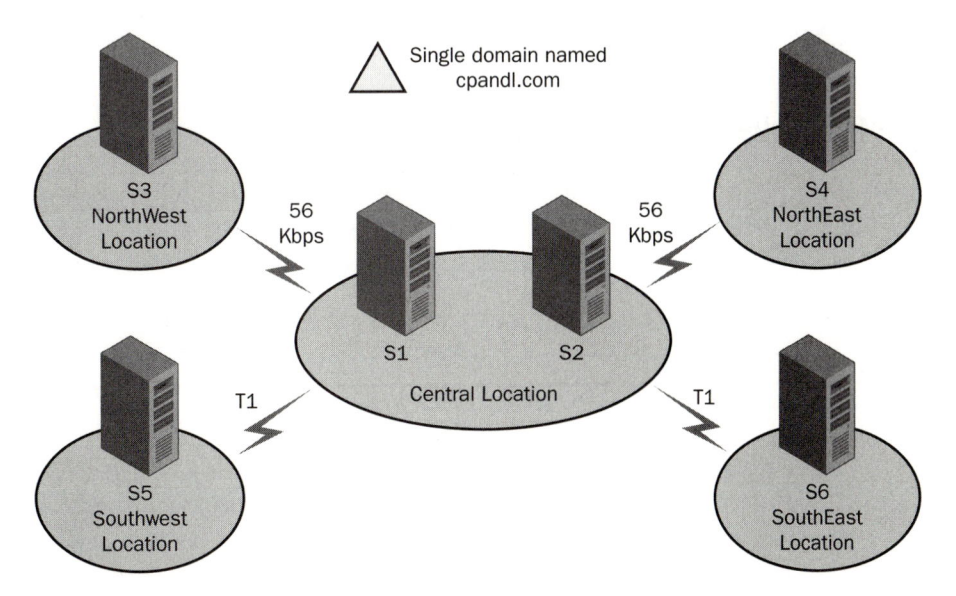

Figure A-1 City Power & Light network infrastructure

S1, S2, S3, S4, S5, and S6 are servers on the City Power & Light network. All of these servers run Microsoft Windows Server 2003, Standard Edition. All client computers run Windows XP Professional. All computers are configured in a single workgroup named WORKGROUP.

Andy Ruth, director of City Power & Light, asks you to design an Active Directory infrastructure for the company. He wants everyone to have single-logon capability. He tells you that all users use the same applications and have roughly equivalent configurations. He thinks the 56 kilobytes per second (Kbps) links are a little slow for the company and he wants to have control over traffic sent across those links. However, he says the T-1 links can handle more traffic without a problem. Andy tells you there are no special security requirements that would require isolating any of the remote locations from the central location.

Based on what you know about the City Power & Light network infrastructure, answer each of the following questions. Include an explanation with your answer.

1. How many forests do you configure for City Power & Light?
2. How many domains do you recommend?
3. What is the minimum number of sites to add?
4. Where would you place global catalog servers or enable universal group membership caching?
5. After you complete your initial configuration, Andy decides that he wants to be able to control replication intervals over all WAN links. How do you change the configuration to accommodate this new request?
6. How do you assign the operations master roles in the Central location?
7. Which domain controller do you configure as the global catalog server in the Central location?
8. Sketch out your proposed configuration based on your answers to the above questions.

TROUBLESHOOTING A BREAK SCENARIO

In this portion of Troubleshooting Lab A, you must resolve a "break" that was introduced by your instructor or lab assistant. The computers you are assigned to fix are in pairs. When you are troubleshooting this issue, consider that the two computers you are troubleshooting are to be configured as shown in Figure A-2.

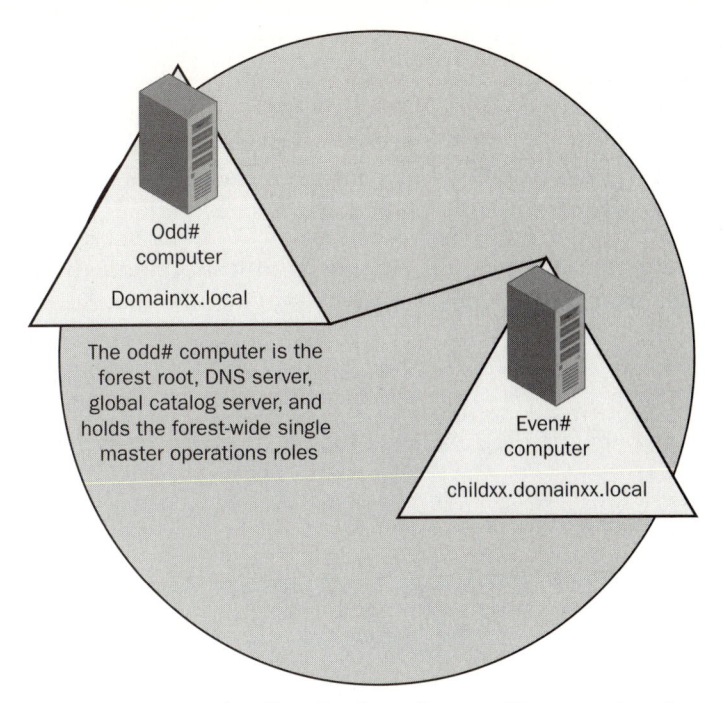

Note: This is the expected configuration for each group of two computers. Any number of configuration errors may be present in your actual lab environment.

Figure A-2 Troubleshooting lab configuration

CAUTION *Do not proceed with break instructions until you receive guidance from your instructor.* *Your instructor or lab assistant will inform you which break scenario you will be performing (Break Scenario 1 or Break Scenario 2) and which computer to use. Your instructor or lab assistant may also have special instructions. Consult with your instructor before proceeding.*

Break Scenario 1

Logging on using the even# computer to the parent domain takes a long time. Administrators are unable to synchronize the child domain using the Repadmin /syncall command. Active Directory administrative consoles do not appear to function properly on the even# computer.

As you resolve the configuration issues, fill out the Troubleshooting Lab Worksheet in the Lab Manual\TroubleshootingLabA folder and include the following information:

- Description of the issue
- A list of all steps taken to try and diagnose the problem, even the ones that did not work
- Description of the problem
- Description of the solution
- List of the resources that you used to help solve this problem

Break Scenario 2

Administrators are unable to synchronize the even# computer with the odd# computer in the Active Directory Sites And Services console. Administrators also are unable to use Repadmin to synchronize the child domain.

As you resolve the configuration issues, fill out the Troubleshooting Lab Worksheet in the Lab Manual\TroubleshootingLabA folder and include the following information:

- Description of the issue
- List of all steps taken to try and diagnose the problem, even the ones that did not work
- Description of the problem
- Description of the solution
- List of the resources that you used to help solve this problem

LAB 5
CREATING AND MANAGING USERS AND GROUPS

This lab contains the following exercises and activities:

- Exercise 5-1: Creating Administrative Accounts
- Exercise 5-2: Testing Administrative Access
- Exercise 5-3: Configuring Groups and Permissions
- Exercise 5-4: Using dsadd to Add a User Account
- Lab Review Questions
- Lab Challenge 5-1: Using dsadd to Add a User Account to the Users Container
- Lab Challenge 5-2: Changing the UPN Suffix with LDIFDE

You are the network administrator of Adventure Works. Adventure Works has a multiple domain Active Directory forest. You manage all network operations. In the near future, you will be adding additional network administrators to help support your organization. Before you begin to assign responsibilities to these new administrators, you want to be sure that you understand what tasks Builtin administrative accounts allow you to perform. You don't want to assign these new administrators more rights than are necessary to perform their assigned roles.

In addition to assigning roles appropriately, you must develop an administrative hierarchy. You know that the company will have many different administrators in the future and you don't want to add them all directly into the domain local or Builtin groups. You want to separate the administrative hierarchy so that you can manage groups of administrators and groups of permissions.

After completing this lab, you will be able to:

- Create administrative user accounts.
- Change primary group memberships.
- Identify which Builtin administrative groups have permissions necessary to:
  - Create sites.
  - Create and manage users.
  - View the Active Directory schema.
  - Modify the Active Directory schema.
- Create global and universal groups and use them to assign permissions to user accounts.
- Use dsadd to add users and organizational units (OUs).
- Make changes to user accounts with LDAP Data Interchange Format Directory Exchange (LDIFDE).

Estimated lesson time: 130 minutes

NOTE *In this lab you will see the characters* **xx**, **yy**, *and* **zz**. *These directions assume that you are working on computers configured in pairs and that each computer has a number. One number is odd and the other number is even. For example, Computer01 is the odd# computer and Computer02 is the even# computer. When you see* **xx**, *substitute the unique number assigned to the odd# computer. When you see* **yy**, *substitute the unique number assigned to the even# computer. When you see* **zz**, *substitute the number assigned to the computer you are working at, either odd or even.*

Whenever you see the Manage Your Server page appear in this lab, select the Don't Display This Page At Logon check box and close the Manage Your Server page.

LAB DEPENDENCIES

In order to complete this lab, you must be sure that the following is done:

- The even# computer must be configured to use the odd# computer as its Preferred DNS Server, as explained in Exercise 1-4.
- Active Directory is installed on the odd# computer. Exercise 2-1 covers the installation of Active Directory on the odd# computer.
- Active Directory is installed on the even# computer. Exercises 2-3 and 2-4 cover the installation of Active Directory on the even# computer.
- Support Tools must be installed, as described in Exercise 3-1.
- Users have the right to log on to domain controllers. Exercise 4-1 explains how to complete this configuration.
- The domain functional level must be Windows 2000 native, which is described in Exercise 4-2.

EXERCISE 5-1: CREATING ADMINISTRATIVE ACCOUNTS

Estimated lesson time: 20 minutes

You are planning to assign new administrators to the Builtin groups for the purpose of creating sites and users, and accessing the Active Directory schema. You must determine which types of Builtin groups give the appropriate levels of access. Before you do this, you must create test user accounts for your experiments.

Creating Administrative Accounts on the Parent Domains

1. On the odd# computer, log on as the default domain administrator of the domain*xx* domain.

2. Open the Active Directory Users And Computers console.

   NOTE To open Active Directory Users And Computers, click Administrative Tools, and then click Active Directory Users And Computers. Alternatively, open the Run dialog box, type **dsa.msc**, and then click OK.

3. Expand the domain object domain*xx*.local in the left window pane, if necessary.

4. In the left window pane, right-click the Users container. Click New, and then click User. The New Object - User dialog box appears.

5. Create a new user account named DomAdmin in the default Users container. In the Full Name text box enter **DomAdmin**.

6. Click the User Logon Name text box, type the same name used in step 5, and then click Next.

7. Type **MSPress#1** in the Password text box and in the Confirm Password text box.

8. Clear the User Must Change Password At Next Logon check box. Click Next, and then click Finish.

9. Ensure that the Users container is selected. In the right window pane of Active Directory Users And Computers, right-click DomAdmin, the user account just created, and click Properties. A DomAdmin Properties dialog box appears.

10. Click the Member Of tab.

11. Click Add. The Select Groups dialog box appears.

12. Type **Dom** in the Enter The Object Name To Select text box. Click Check Names. The Multiple Names Found dialog box appears. From the multiple names listed click Domain Admins, and then click OK. Domain Admins is underlined in the Select Groups dialog box. Click OK. The Select Groups dialog box closes.

    NOTE A Multiple Names Found dialog box appears only when you click Check Names and there is more than one match to the query.

> **TIP** The more information you can provide when checking names, the smaller the list of matching names found.

13. In the DomAdmin Properties dialog box, click Domain Admins in the Member Of selection box. Click Set Primary Group to make the primary group Domain Admins.

14. Click Domain Users in the Member Of selection box. Click Remove to make Domain Admins the only group membership for this user account. A Remove User From Group text message appears. Read the message, and click Yes.

15. Click OK in the DomAdmin Properties dialog box.

16. Use a similar technique to create two additional accounts named SchAdmin and EntAdmin. Ensure that the SchAdmin account is a member only of the Schema Admins group and that the EntAdmin account is a member only of the Enterprise Admins group.

Creating Administrative Accounts on the Child Domain

1. On the even# computer, log on as the default administrator of the child*xx* domain.

2. Open the Active Directory Users And Computers console.

   > **NOTE** To open Active Directory Users And Computers, click Administrative Tools, and then click Active Directory Users And Computers. Alternatively, open the Run dialog box, type **dsa.msc**, and then click OK.

3. Expand the domain object, child*xx*.domain*xx*.local, in the left window pane.

4. In the left window pane, right-click the Users container. Click New, and then click User. The New Object - User dialog box appears.

5. Create a new user account named DomAdmin in the default Users container. Click the Full Name text box and enter **DomAdmin**.

6. Click the User Logon Name text box, type the same name used in step 5, and then click Next.

7. Type **MSPress#1** in the Password text box and in the Confirm Password text box.

8. Clear the User Must Change Password At Next Logon check box. Click Next, and then click Finish.

9. Ensure that the Users container is selected. In the right window pane of Active Directory Users And Computers, right-click DomAdmin, the user account just created, and click Properties. A DomAdmin Properties dialog box appears.

10. Click the Member Of tab.

11. Click Add. The Select Groups dialog box appears.

12. Type **Dom** in the Enter The Objects Name To Select text box. Click Check Names. The Multiple Names Found dialog box appears. From the multiple names listed, click Domain Admins, and then click OK. Domain Admins is underlined in the Select Groups dialog box. Click OK. The Select Groups dialog box closes.

    NOTE A Multiple Names Found dialog box appears only when you click Check Names and there is more than one match to the query.

    TIP The more information you can provide when checking names, the smaller the list of matching names found.

13. In the DomAdmin Properties dialog box, click Domain Admins in the Member Of selection box. Click Set Primary Group to make the primary group Domain Admins.

14. Click Domain Users in the Member Of selection box. Click Remove to make Domain Admins the only group membership for this user account. A Remove User From Group text message appears. Read the message, and click Yes.

15. Click OK in the DomAdmin Properties dialog box.

16. Use the techniques that you used in steps 4 through 8 to create two additional user accounts named SchAdmin and EntAdmin. Do not configure group memberships for these accounts, that will be done in the next part of this exercise using the odd# computer.

Adding Child User Accounts to Enterprise-Wide Administrative Roles

1. On the odd# computer return to the Active Directory Users And Computers console.

2. Ensure that the Users container is selected. Right-click the Enterprise Admins group in the right window pane, and then click Properties. An Enterprise Admins Properties dialog box appears.

3. Click the Members tab, and then click Add. The Select Users, Contacts, Computers, Or Groups dialog box appears.

4. Click Locations. The Locations dialog box appears.

5. Expand the domain*xx*.local object and then expand the child*xx*.domain*xx*.local object.

6. Click the Users container under the child domain, and click OK.

7. Type **ENT** in the Enter The Object Name To Select text box of the Select Users, Contacts, Computers, Or Groups dialog box, click Check Names. The EntAdmin group from the child domain should be displayed, as shown in the following figure. Click OK.

[Screenshot of Enterprise Admins Properties and Select Users, Contacts, Computers, or Groups dialog boxes]

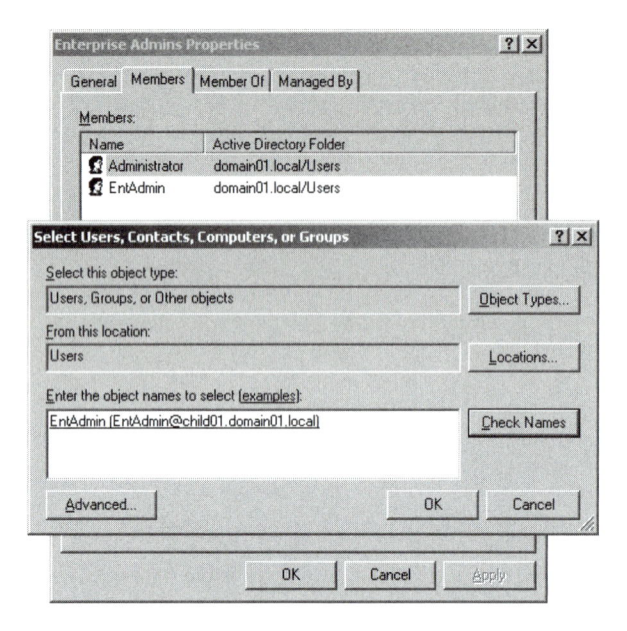

8. Click OK on the Enterprise Admins Properties dialog box.

9. Use a similar technique to add the SchAdmin user account from the child*xx* domain to the Schema Admins group on the parent domain.

10. On both computers, close all open windows and log off.

EXERCISE 5-2: TESTING ADMINISTRATIVE ACCESS

Estimated completion time: 40 minutes

You must now test the capabilities of each of the user accounts you created in the previous exercise.

Which Accounts Can Create Sites?

Use the administrative accounts created in Exercise 5-1, that is, DomAdmin, SchAdmin and EntAdmin, to complete this activity.

> **NOTE** The administration tools might not show on the Start menu for some of the administrative accounts. When this happens, you can access Active Directory Sites And Services by clicking Start, clicking Run, typing **dssite.msc** in the Open text box, and clicking OK.

1. Log on using the user account being tested, such as DomAdmin. On the odd# computer, log on to the domain*xx* domain. On the even# computer, log on to the child*xx* domain.

2. Using Active Directory Sites And Services, attempt to create a site. Try to create a unique site name with each administrative account, and write down the names of the accounts that can be used to create a new site. Refer to Exercise 3-3 if you need directions for creating a site.

QUESTION Which administrative user accounts can create a site on the domain of which they are members?

3. If a site is created successfully, delete the site. In the left window pane of Active Directory Sites And Services, right-click the site name, and click Delete. An Active Directory message appears. Read the message, and click Yes to confirm you want to delete the site. Another Active Directory message box appears. Read the message, and click Yes to confirm.

Which Accounts Can Create Users?

Use the administrative accounts created in Exercise 5-1, that is, DomAdmin, SchAdmin and EntAdmin, to complete this activity.

NOTE The administration tools might not show on the Start menu on some of the administrative accounts. When this happens, you can access Active Directory Users And Computers by clicking Start, clicking Run, typing **dsa.msc** in the Open text box, and clicking OK.

1. Log on using the user account being tested, such as DomAdmin. On the odd# computer, log on to the domain*xx* domain. On the even# computer, log on to the child*xx* domain.

2. Using Active Directory Users And Computers, attempt to create a unique user account on the local domain. Write down the names of the accounts that can be used to create new users.

3. Using Active Directory Users And Computers, attempt to create a unique user account on the opposite domain. In the left window pane of the Active Directory Users And Computers console, right-click the Active Directory Users And Computers object and select Connect To Domain. The Connect To Domain dialog box appears.

4. Click Browse. In the Browse For Domain dialog box, select the opposite domain, as shown in the following figure.

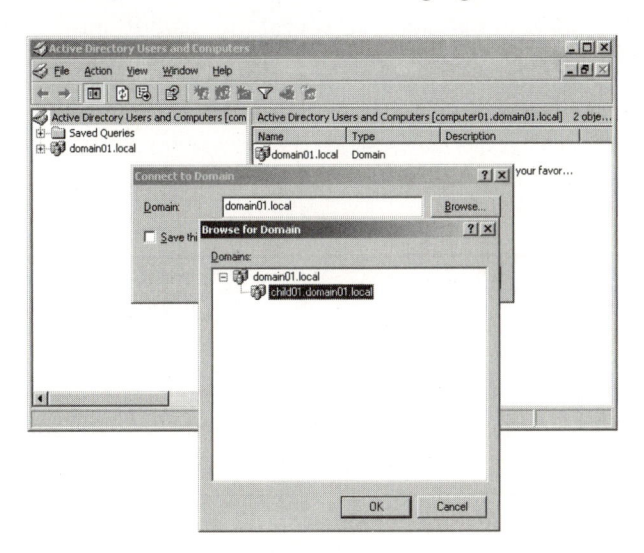

5. Click OK. Ensure the Save This Domain Setting For The Current Console check box is not checked and click OK.

6. In the opposite domain, attempt to create a unique user account. Write down the names of the accounts that can be used to create new users.

   QUESTION Which administrative user accounts can create users on the parent and child domains?

7. Close the Active Directory Users And Computers console and log off.

Which Accounts Can Manage the Schema?

Use the administrative accounts created in Exercise 5-1, that is, DomAdmin, SchAdmin and EntAdmin, to complete this activity.

1. On the odd# computer, log on as the DomAdmin user of the domain*xx* domain. On the even# computer, log on as the DomAdmin user of the child*xx* domain.

2. Register the schmmgmt.dll. Open the Run dialog box and type **regsvr32 schmmgmt.dll** and press Enter. Click OK in the message box indicating the registration succeeded.

3. Add the Active Directory Schema snap-in to Microsoft Management Console (MMC). Open the Run dialog box. Type **MMC** in the Open text box, and click OK. The MMC console appears.

4. Add the Active Directory Schema snap-in. Click File, and then click Add/Remove Snap-In. The Add/Remove Snap-In box appears.

5. Click Add. The Add Standalone Snap-In dialog box appears.

6. Locate and click the Active Directory Schema snap-in.

7. Click Add, and then click Close.

8. Click OK on the Add/Remove Snap-In dialog box.

9. Expand the Active Directory Schema object to reveal the Classes and Attributes nodes.

10. Click Attributes. You should see a list of schema attributes appear in the right window pane.

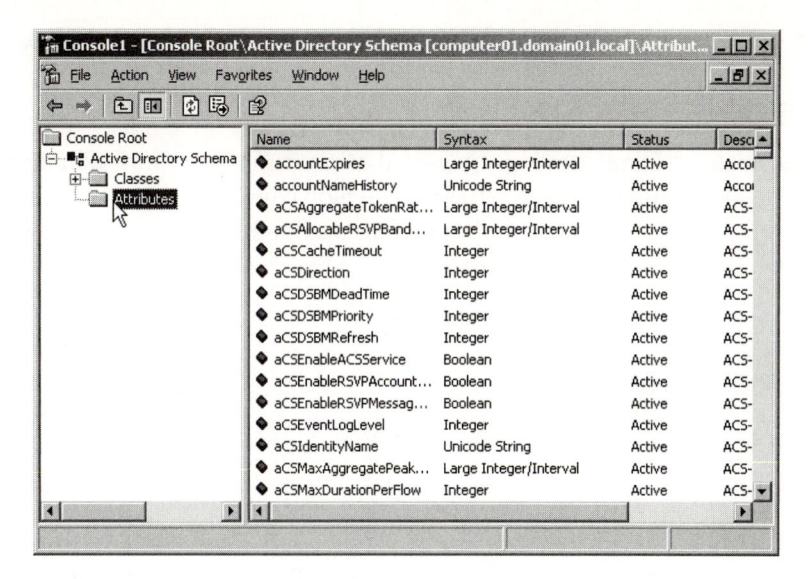

11. Right-click the Attributes object. If you see the option to Create Attribute is grayed out in the context menu, then this user account does not have the ability to modify the schema.

12. Click the File menu and then click Save As.

13. Type **C:\schema.msc** in the File Name text box. Click Save and close the Schema console.

14. Log off.

15. Log on as the SchAdmin user of the local domain.

16. Open the Run dialog box and type **C:\schema.msc** in the Open text box and click OK. The Schema console should open.

17. If you can see the list of Active Directory Schema attributes, the user account has the ability to view the schema.

18. Right-click the Attributes object and if you see that the Create Attribute option is available in the context menu, the user account has the ability to modify the schema.

19. Log off and log on as the EntAdmin user. Repeat steps 16-18, then log off and answer the following questions.

    QUESTION Which administrative user accounts can view the Schema attributes using the Active Directory Schema snap-in?

    QUESTION Which administrative user accounts can create a new attribute in the Active Directory schema?

EXERCISE 5-3: CONFIGURING GROUPS AND PERMISSIONS

Estimated completion time: 15 minutes

You must now create an administrative structure that you can use for new administrators. You want to group administrators into separate global groups. Then you want to create a universal group that can be used to give new administrators permissions equivalent to the local administrators of each domain.

Creating Global Groups

1. On the odd# computer, log on as the default administrator of the domain*xx* domain.

2. Open the Active Directory Users And Computers console.

3. Expand the domain*xx*.local domain, and then right-click the Users container.

4. Click New, and then click Group. The New Object – Group dialog box appears. Notice the following figure shows that the Group Scope default is Global and the Group Type default is Security. Keep these default settings.

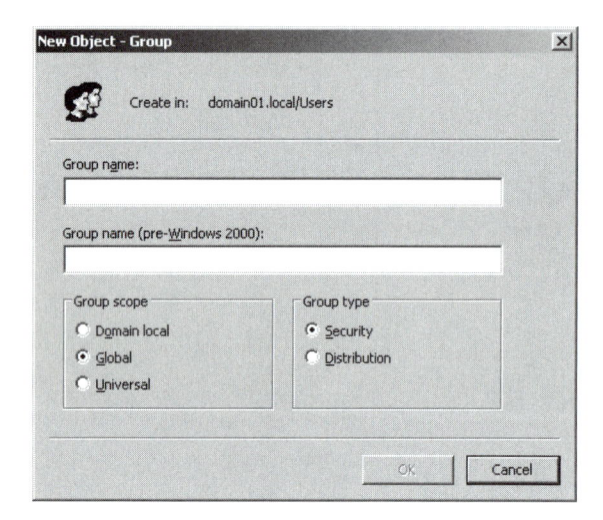

5. Type **LAdmins*xx*** in the Group Name text box, and click OK.

6. On the even# computer, log on as the default administrator of the child*xx* domain.

7. Open the Active Directory Users And Computers console.

8. Expand the child*xx*.domain*xx*.local domain, and then right-click the Users container.

9. Click New, and then click Group. The New Object – Group dialog box appears. Notice the Group Scope default is Global and the Group Type default is Security. Keep these default settings.

10. Type **LAdmins*yy*** in the Group Name text box, and click OK.

Creating Universal Groups

1. On the odd# computer, right-click the Users container.
2. Click New, and then click Group. The New Object – Group dialog box appears.
3. Type **LAdmins** in the Group Name text box.
4. In the Group Scope area, select the Universal radio button, leave the Group Type set to Security, and click OK.
5. Ensure that the Users container is selected. In the right window pane of Active Directory Users And Computers, right-click LAdmins, and click Properties.
6. Click the Members tab, and click Add. The Select Users, Contacts, Computers, Or Groups dialog box appears.
7. Type **LAdmins*xx*** in the Enter The Object Names To Select text box, and then click OK. LAdmins*xx* is a global group.
8. Click Add again. The Select Users, Contacts, Computers, Or Groups dialog box appears again.
9. Click Locations. The Locations dialog box appears.
10. Expand the parent domain, and then expand the child domain.
11. Click the Users container under the child domain, and click OK.
12. Type **LAdmins*yy*** in Enter The Object Names To Select text box, and click OK. LAdmins*yy* is a global group.
13. Click the Member Of tab, and click Add. The Select Groups dialog box appears.
14. Type **Administrators** in the Enter The Object Names To Select text box, and click OK.
15. Click Add again. The Select Groups dialog box appears.
16. Click Locations. The Locations dialog box appears.
17. Expand the parent domain.
18. Click the child domain and click OK.
19. Type **Administrators** in the Enter The Object Names To Select text box, and click OK.
20. Click OK in the LAdmins Properties dialog box.

Assigning Permissions Through Group Membership

1. On the odd# computer, create a user account named LocalAdmin*xx* on the parent domain. Refer to Exercise 5-1, Creating Administrative Accounts on the Parent Domain.

2. Make the LocalAdmin*xx* user a member of the LAdmins*xx* group.

3. On the even# computer, create a user account named LocalAdmin*yy* on the child domain. Refer to Exercise 5-1, Creating Administrative Accounts on the Child Domain.

4. Make the LocalAdmin*yy* user a member of the LAdmins*yy* group.

5. Log off and log on to each computer with its newly created user account.

    QUESTION *Can you perform administrative tasks, such as create a user account, shut down the server, or set the time, on the domain controllers? Explain the group membership chain that provides this user account with its current permissions.*

6. Log off both computers.

EXERCISE 5-4: USING DSADD TO ADD A USER ACCOUNT

Estimated completion time: 10 minutes

Your organization is growing and you need to add new OUs and users.

Using dsadd to Create an OU and User in the Parent Domain

A Sales department was added to your organizational structure and you decide to create a new OU to help you manage the resources of this new department. Additionally, a new manager, Kelly Blue, was just hired for the Sales department. You must create a user account for Kelly in the new OU. You want to use dsadd to add these new objects.

1. On the odd# computer, log on as the default administrator of the domain*xx* domain.

2. Open a command prompt window.

3. Type **dsadd ou ou=Sales,dc=domain*xx*,dc=local -desc Lab5** in the command prompt window, and press Enter.

4. Type **dsadd user cn=Kelly,ou=Sales,dc=domain*xx*,dc=local -pwd MSPress#1 -samid KellyB -upn Kelly@domain*xx*.local** in the command prompt window, and press Enter.

5. Open the Active Directory Users And Computers console, and verify that the Sales OU exists, and the Kelly user account exists inside the OU.

Using dsadd to Create an OU and User in the Child Domain

A Service department was added to your organizational structure and you decide to create a new OU to help manage the resources of this new department. Additionally, a new manager, Jeff Hay, was just hired for the Service department. You must create a user account for Jeff in the new OU. You want to use dsadd to add these new objects.

1. On the even# computer, log on as the default administrator of the child*xx* domain.

2. Open a command prompt window.

3. Type **dsadd ou ou=Service,dc=child*xx*,dc=domain*xx*,dc=local -desc Lab5** in the command prompt window and press Enter.

4. Type **dsadd user cn=Jeff,ou=Service,dc=child*xx*,dc=domain*xx*, dc=local -pwd MSPress#1 -samid JeffH -upn jeff@child*xx*.domain*xx*.local** in the command prompt window, and press Enter.

    NOTE Notice that you can set an initial password with the dsadd command. You cannot set an initial password with Comma-Separated Value Directory Exchange (CSVDE) or LDIFDE. However, you can modify a password created with LDIFDE. For more information on LDIFDE, visit Microsoft Knowledge Base article Q263991, "How to set a users password with LDIFDE," available at http://support.microsoft.com.

5. Open the Active Directory Users And Computers console, verify that the Service OU exists, and the Jeff user account exists inside the OU.

LAB REVIEW QUESTIONS

Estimated completion time: 15 minutes

1. In your words, describe what you learned during this lab.

2. What can you do with dsadd when creating user accounts that are not available with CSVDE and LDIFDE?

3. Name a task that a member of Schema Admins cannot perform that a member of either Enterprise Admins or Domain Admins can perform.

4. What command must you run before you can add the Active Directory Schema console as a snap-in to Microsoft Management Console?

5. What type of administrative membership allows you to add attributes and object classes to the Active Directory database?

LAB CHALLENGE 5-1: USING DSADD TO ADD A USER ACCOUNT TO THE USERS CONTAINER

Estimated completion time: 10 minutes

Amy Lyon and Ben Smith are new employees. You want to use dsadd to create user accounts for them in the appropriate domain.

Task 1: On the odd# computer, use dsadd to create a user account for Amy Lyon in the Users container of the domain*xx* domain. Amy's username should be Amy and her pre–Windows 2000 username should be AmyL. Her User Principle Name (UPN) should be Amy@cohowinery.com. Set her password to MSPress#1.

Task 2: On the even# computer, use dsadd to create a user account for Ben Smith in the Users container of the child*xx* domain. Ben's user logon name should be Ben and his pre–Windows 2000 user logon name should be BenS. Set his password to MSPress#1. His UPN should be Ben@cohovineyard.com.

LAB CHALLENGE 5-2: CHANGING THE UPN SUFFIX WITH LDIFDE

Estimated completion time: 20 minutes

Amy and Ben say they need the UPN suffix contoso.com. They want to be able to log on as Amy@contoso.com and Ben@contoso.com, respectively.

Task: Modify the accounts you created for Amy and Ben using an LDIFDE file to change the UPN. Create one file to be used on the odd# computer to modify Amy's account. Create another file to be used on the even# computer to modify Ben's account.

LAB 6
EMPLOYING SECURITY CONCEPTS

This lab contains the following exercises and activities:

- Exercise 6-1: Using Naming Standards and Secure Passwords
- Exercise 6-2: Employing Administrator Account Security
- Exercise 6-3: Delegating Administrative Responsibility
- Exercise 6-4: Hiding a User Account
- Lab Review Questions
- Lab Challenge 6-1: Using Dsmove
- Lab Challenge 6-2: Moving an OU with Movetree
- Lab Challenge 6-3: Moving a User with Movetree

You are a network administrator of Adventure Works, which has a single Active Directory domain model with four sites named Greece, Malaysia, Thailand, and Arizona. The Arizona site has three domain controllers, and each of the other sites has one domain controller. The domain uses Active Directory–integrated Domain Name System (DNS), and all domain controllers have the DNS service installed.

The forest root domain is named adventure-works.com. Adventure Works headquarters is located in Tempe, Arizona, in the United States. The company also has locations on Penang Island in Malaysia, Samui Island in Thailand, and Santorini Island in Greece.

The Tempe location has three domain controllers and 250 user accounts. The main administrative functions are performed at this location. Top-level organizational units (OUs) include Accounting, Marketing, and Operations. The Accounting OU has two subordinate OUs named Accounts Payable and Accounts Receivable. The Marketing OU has two subordinate OUs named Sales and Customer Service. The Production OU has three subordinate OUs named Penang, Samui, and Santorini.

Recently, a consulting group performed an audit on the adventure-works.com domain. The consulting group recommended several organization and security changes. You've been assigned by your manager to perform the following tasks.

LAB 6: EMPLOYING SECURITY CONCEPTS

After completing this lab, you will be able to:

- Implement a standard naming scheme for user accounts throughout the entire company.
- Educate users on configuring secure passwords.
- Educate other administrators on how to reduce administrative account exposure.
- Delegate permissions appropriately to department managers.
- Implement user naming standards.
- Configure Alt character passwords.
- Use the Runas program.
- Use the Delegation Of Control Wizard.
- Modify the Access Control List (ACL) of an OU to hide the contents.
- Move OUs and user accounts.

Estimated completion time: 120 minutes

> **NOTE** In this lab, you will see the characters **xx**, **yy**, and **zz**. These directions assume you are working on computers configured in pairs and that each computer has a number. One number is odd and the other number is even. For example, Computer01 is the odd# computer and Computer02 is the even# computer. When you see **xx**, substitute the unique number assigned to the odd# computer. When you see **yy**, substitute the unique number assigned to the even# computer. When you see **zz**, substitute the number assinged to the computer you are working at, either odd or even.
>
> Whenever you see the Manage Your Server page appear in this lab, select the Don't Display This Page At Logon check box and close the Manage Your Server page.

LAB DEPENDENCIES

In order to complete this lab, you must be sure that the following is done:

- Active Directory is installed on the odd# computer. Exercise 2-1 covers the installation of Active Directory on the odd# computer.
- Active Directory is installed on the even# computer. Exercises 2-3 and 2-4 cover the installation of Active Directory on the even# computer.
- Users have the right to log on to domain controllers. Exercise 4-1 explains how to complete this configuration.

EXERCISE 6-1: USING NAMING STANDARDS AND SECURE PASSWORDS

Estimated completion time: 5 minutes

Company policy states that each employee's user account name must be created from the employee's first initial of their first name, entire last name, and their employee identification number. All employees' passwords will be complex and include characters from the alternate character set.

NOTE You can create the ☺ (smiling face) character by enabling the NUM LOCK feature on your keyboard. Hold down the ALT key and use the keypad to enter the number 1. If you don't have a keypad, you should be able to create this character by using the number row at the top of your keyboard, once you enable NUM LOCK. If you are still unable to use Alt character passwords, substitute a regular number 1 for this part.

Creating User Accounts with Alternate Character Passwords on Both Domains

1. On the odd# computer, log on as the default administrator of the domain*xx* domain.

2. Use the Active Directory Users And Computers console to create a user account based on your name in the Users container. Use the naming standards described in the scenario for this exercise. Substitute the odd# computer number for the employee identification number. For example, a user named Terry Adams who is using Computer01 would have the following values:

   NOTE Be sure to use the Active Directory Users And Computers console to create this user account. You will not be able to create the user accounts with alternate character passwords from a command prompt window.

First Name	Terry
Last Name	Adams
Full Name	Terry Adams
Logon Name	TAdams01
Password	MSPress#☺

   Clear the User Must Change Password At Next Logon check box.

3. On the even# computer, log on as the default administrator of the child*xx* domain.

4. Use the Active Directory Users And Computers console to create a user account based on your name in the Users container. Use the naming standards described in the scenario for this exercise. Substitute the even# computer number for the employee identification number. For example, a user named Jeff Pike who is using Computer02 would have the logon name JPike02. The password should be MSPress#☺. Clear the User Must Change Password At Next Logon check box.

5. Log off both computers.

EXERCISE 6-2: EMPLOYING ADMINISTRATOR ACCOUNT SECURITY

Estimated completion time: 20 minutes

You must demonstrate the various methods for using the Runas utility to administrators to reduce the exposure of administrative accounts.

Using Runas at the Command Prompt Window

1. Log on to each computer using the user accounts you created in Exercise 6-1.

2. Open the Active Directory Users And Computers console.

   NOTE To open Active Directory Users And Computers, open the Run dialog box, type **dsa.msc**, and then click OK.

3. Try to reset your password. Click the Users container in the left window pane. In the right window pane, right-click your user account, and click Reset Password. A Reset Password dialog box appears. Type **MSPress#1** in the password boxes, and click OK. A message box appears. Read the message and click OK.

   QUESTION Why does this operation fail?

4. Close the Active Directory Users And Computers console.

5. On the odd# computer, open a command prompt window, type **Runas /user:administrator@domain*xx*.local "mmc dsa.msc"**, and press ENTER.

6. On the even# computer, open a command prompt window. Type **Runas /user:administrator@child*xx*.domain*xx*.local "mmc dsa.msc"** and press ENTER.

7. When you are prompted for the password, type **MSPress#1**, and press ENTER. Wait a few seconds and the Active Directory Users And Computers console appears.

8. Try to reset your password. Click the Users container in the left window pane. In the right window pane, right-click your user account, and click Reset Password. A Reset Password dialog box appears. Type **MSPress#1** in the password boxes, and click OK. A message box appears.

   QUESTION Why were you successful this time?

9. Click OK.

10. Close the the Active Directory Users And Computers console and the command prompt window.

Using Runas from the Run Dialog Box

You need to open the Active Directory Sites And Services console using a user account that is a member of the Enterprise Admins group.

1. From either computer, open the Run dialog box.

2. Type **Runas /user:administrator@domain.xx.local "mmc dssite.msc"** and press ENTER. A command prompt window appears.

3. Type **MSPress#1** in the command prompt window, and press ENTER. The Active Directory Sites And Services console appears.

4. As a user with Enterprise Admin permissions, you should have the ability to create a new site (reference Exercise 3-3). If you do create a site, delete it. Then, close the Active Directory Sites And Services console.

Creating and Using a Runas Shortcut

You want to create a shortcut on your desktop that will allow you to easily manage your domains and forest without necessitating you to log off when using your domain user account.

1. Find an area of the desktop where there are no icons, and right-click that area.

2. Click New, and then click Shortcut. A Create Shortcut Wizard appears.

3. Type **Runas /user:administrator@domain.xx.local "mmc domain.msc"** in the Type The Location Of The Item text box, and click Next.

4. Type **Domains and Trusts** in the Type A Name For This Shortcut text box, and click Finish.

5. Double-click the icon on the desktop named Domains And Trusts. A command prompt window appears.

6. Type **MSPress#1** in the command prompt window, and press ENTER. The Active Directory Domains And Trust console appears.

7. Close the console.

Attempting to Run Multiple Runas Consoles Simultaneously

You want to see if you can run multiple consoles simultaneously with the Runas utility.

1. On either computer, open the Run dialog box.

2. Type **Runas /user:administrator@domain.xx.local "mmc dsa.msc"** and press ENTER. A command prompt window appears.

3. Type **MSPress#1** in the command prompt window, and press ENTER. The Active Directory Users And Computers console appears.

4. Open the Run dialog box.

5. Type **Runas /user:administrator@domain*xx*.local "mmc dssite.msc"** and press ENTER. A command prompt window appears.

6. Type **MSPress#1** in the command prompt window, and press ENTER. The Active Directory Sites And Services console appears.

7. Open the Run dialog box.

8. Type **Runas /user:administrator@domain*xx*.local "mmc domain.msc"** and press ENTER. A command prompt window appears.

9. Type **MSPress#1** in the command prompt window, and press ENTER. The Active Directory Domains And Trusts console appears.

10. Close all open consoles and log off the computer.

EXERCISE 6-3: DELEGATING ADMINISTRATIVE RESPONSIBILITY

Estimated completion time: 25 minutes

You must assign the ability to reset passwords to the manager of a new department.

Delegating Control on the Parent Domain

1. On the odd# computer, log on as the default administrator of the domain*xx* domain.

2. Open the Run dialog box. Type **"C:\Lab Manual \Lab06\L6Pusers.bat"** and press ENTER. This batch file creates three users (User1, User2, and Manager) in the Users container.

3. Open the Active Directory Users And Computers console.

4. Right-click the domain*xx* local object in the left window pane, click New, and then click Organizational Unit (OU). A New Object Organizational Unit dialog box appears.

5. Type **Mgmt1** in the name text box, and click OK.

6. In the left window pane of the Users And Computers console, right-click the Mgmt1 OU, and click Delegate Control. The Delegation Of Control Wizard appears.

7. Click Next. The Users Or Groups page appears.

8. Click Add. The Select Users, Computers, Or Groups dialog box appears.

9. Type **Manager** in the Enter The Object Names To Select text box, and click Check Names. Click OK and the Users Or Groups page should be similar to the following figure.

[Screenshot of Delegation of Control Wizard - Users or Groups page showing Manager (DOMAIN01\Manager) selected]

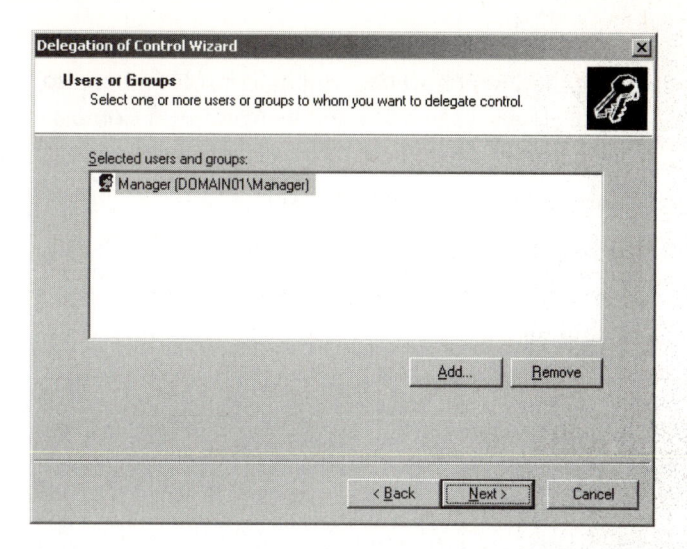

10. In the Users Or Groups page, click Next. The Tasks To Delegate page appears.

11. Select the Reset User Passwords And Force Password Change At Next Logon check box, and then click Next. Click Finish.

12. Move the User1 account from the Users container to the Mgmt1 OU. You can use the drag-and-drop method to move the user account. You can also right-click the user account and then click Move. A Move dialog box opens. Select the OU to which you want to move the user and then click OK.

13. Open a command prompt. Type **dsmove cn=user2,cn=users, dc=domain*xx*,dc=local -newparent ou=Mgmt1,dc=domain*xx*,dc=local** and press ENTER.

14. In the left window pane of Active Directory Users And Computers, select the Mgmt1 OU. Refresh the display by clicking Refresh on the Action menu or pressing F5. User1 and User2 should appear in the right window pane.

15. Close the command prompt window, close the Active Directory Users And Computers console, and log off the computer.

Delegating Control on the Child Domain

1. On the even# computer, log on as the default administrator of the child*xx* domain.

2. Open the Run dialog box. Type **"C:\Lab Manual\Lab06\L6Cusers.bat"** and press ENTER. This batch file creates three users (User3, User4, and Manager) in the Users container.

3. Open the Active Directory Users And Computers console.

4. Right-click the child*xx*.domain*xx*.local object in the left window pane, click New, and then click Organizational Unit (OU). A New Object Organizational Unit dialog box appears.

5. Type **Mgmt2** in the Name text box, and click OK.

6. In the left window pane of the Users And Computers console, right-click the Mgmt2 OU, and click Delegate Control. The Delegation Of Control Wizard appears.

7. Click Next. The Users Or Groups page appears.

8. Click Add. A Select Users, Computers, Or Groups dialog box appears.

9. Type **Manager** in the Enter The Object Names To Select text box, and click Check Names. Click OK.

10. In the Users Or Groups page, click Next. The Tasks To Delegate page appears.

11. Select the Reset User Passwords And Force Password Change At Next Logon check box, and then click Next. Click Finish.

12. Move the User3 account from the Users container to the Mgmt2 OU. You can use the drag-and-drop method to move the user account. You can also right-click the user account and then click Move. A Move dialog box opens. Select the OU to which you want to move the user and then click OK.

13. Open a command prompt window. Type **dsmove cn=user4,cn=users,dc=child*xx*,dc=domain*xx*,dc=local -newparent ou=Mgmt2,dc=child*xx*,dc=domain*xx*,dc=local** and press ENTER.

14. In the left window pane of Active Directory Users And Computers, select the Mgmt2 OU. Refresh the display by clicking Refresh on the Action menu or pressing F5. User3 and User4 should appear in the right window pane as shown in the following figure.

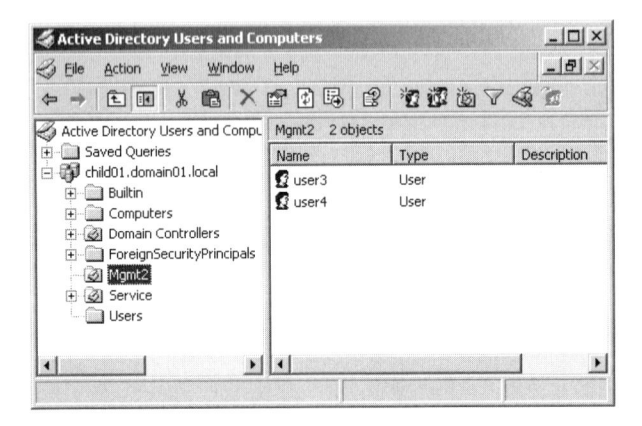

15. Close the command prompt window, close the Active Directory Users And Computers console, and log off the computer.

Testing Delegated Permissions on the Parent Domain

1. On the odd# computer, log on using the Manager user account in the domain*xx* domain. The password is MSPress#1.

2. Open the Active Directory Users And Computers console.

3. In the left window pane, expand the domain*xx*.local object and click the Mgmt1 OU.

4. In the right window pane, right-click User2, and click Reset Password. The Reset Password dialog box appears.

5. Type **MSPress#☺** in the New Password text box and in the Confirm Password text box, and then click OK. The Active Directory message box appears verifying that the user's password has changed. Click OK.

6. In the right window pane, right-click User1, and click Delete.

7. An Active Directory warning message appears asking you to confirm the deletion of the account. Click Yes.

8. The Active Directory message box appears telling you that you do not have sufficient privileges to delete the user account. Click OK.

    QUESTION Why can the manager change a user's password on the Mgmt1 OU but cannot delete a user's account?

9. Try changing the password for another user account that is not a member of the Mgmt1 OU; for example, the Administrator account in the Users container.

    QUESTION Is the manager account able to change an account password outside the OU?

10. Close the Active Directory Users And Computers console and log off the computer.

Testing Delegated Permissions on the Child Domain

1. On the even# computer, log on using the Manager user account in the child*xx* domain. The password is MSPress#1.

2. Open the Active Directory Users And Computers console.

3. In the left window pane, expand the child*xx*.domain*xx*.local object and click the Mgmt2 OU.

4. In the right window pane, right-click User4, and click Reset Password. The Reset Password dialog box appears.

5. Type **MSPress#☺** in the New Password text box and in the Confirm Password text box, and then click OK. The Active Directory message box appears verifying that the user's password was changed. Click OK.

6. In the right window pane, right-click User3, and click Delete. The Active Directory message box appears asking you to confirm the deletion of the object. Click Yes.

7. The Active Directory message box appears telling you that you do not have sufficient privileges to delete the user account. Click OK.

   QUESTION *Why can the manager change a user's password on the Mgmt2 OU, but cannot delete a user's account?*

8. Try changing the password for another user account that is not a member of the Mgmt2 OU; for example, the Administrator account in the Users container.

   QUESTION *Is the manager account able to change an account password outside the OU?*

9. Close the Active Directory Users And Computers console and log off the computer.

EXERCISE 6-4: HIDING A USER ACCOUNT

Estimated completion time: 15 minutes

Your manager wants to prevent users from finding objects in certain OUs. Your manager asks you to prepare a demonstration for other administrators to show them how objects can be hidden from directory searches.

Finding a User in Active Directory from the Parent Domain

1. On the odd# computer, log on using the user account from Exercise 6-1 for the domain*xx* domain.

2. Click Start, and click Search. A Search Results window appears.

3. Expand the Search Results window.

4. In the left window pane, click Other Search Options, click Printers, Computers, Or People, and then click People In Your Address Book. The Find People dialog box appears.

5. In the Look In selection box, select Active Directory from the list, as shown in the following graphic.

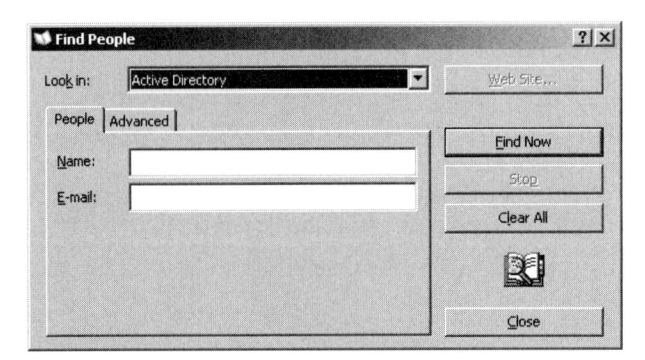

6. Type **User1** in the Name text box, and click Find Now.

    QUESTION How many users do you find with the username User1?

7. Close the Find People dialog box and the Search Results window. You must complete this step or the search results will remain cached.

Finding a User in Active Directory from the Child Domain

1. On the even# computer, log on using the user account credentials from Exercise 6-1 for the child*xx* domain.
2. Click Start, and click Search. A Search Results window appears.
3. Expand the Search Results window.
4. In the left window pane click Other Search Options, click Printers, Computers, Or People, and then click People In Your Address Book. The Find People dialog box appears.
5. In the Look In selection box, select Active Directory from the list displayed.
6. Type **User3** in the Name text box, and click Find Now.

    QUESTION How many users do you find with the username User3?

7. Close the Find People dialog box and the Search Results window. You must complete this step or the search results will remain cached.

Resetting Permission for Mgmt1

1. On the odd# computer, open the Run dialog box.
2. Type **runas /user:administrator@domain*xx*.local "mmc dsa.msc"** in the Open text box, and click OK. A command prompt window opens.
3. Type **MSPress#1** into the command prompt window, and press ENTER. The Active Directory Users And Computers console appears.
4. Click the View menu, and then click Advanced Features. Click the View menu again and ensure there is a check mark next to the Advanced Features option. If not, click that option again.
5. In the left window pane, expand the domain*xx*.local object and right-click Mgmt1, and then click Properties. The Mgmt1 Properties dialog box appears.
6. Click the Security tab.
7. In the Group Or User Names area, click Authenticated Users.
8. In the Permissions For Authenticated Users area, clear Allow Read permission.
9. Click Advanced. An Advanced Security Settings For Mgmt1 dialog box appears.

10. Clear the Allow Inheritable Permissions check box. As shown in the following graphic, a Security message appears.

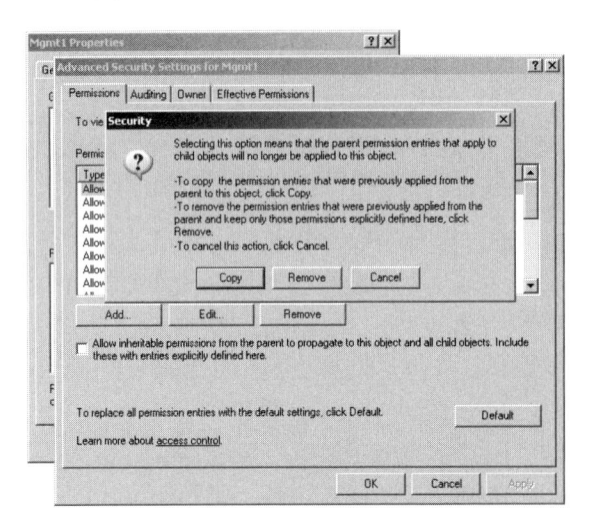

11. Read the message, and click Remove.
12. Click OK in the Advanced Security Settings For Mgmt1 dialog box.
13. Click OK in the Mgmt1 Properties dialog box.
14. Close the Active Directory Users And Computers console.

Resetting Permission for Mgmt2

1. On the even# computer, open the Run dialog box.
2. Type **runas /user:administrator@child*xx*.domain*xx*.local "mmc dsa.msc"** in the Open text box, and click OK. A command prompt window opens.

    NOTE Be sure to include "childxx" in the Runas command.

3. Type **MSPress#1** in the command prompt window, and press ENTER. The Active Directory Users And Computers console appears.
4. Click the View menu and then click Advanced Features. Click the View menu again and ensure there is a check mark next to the Advanced Features option. If not, click that option again.
5. In the left window pane, expand the child*xx*.domain*xx*.local object and right-click Mgmt2, and then click Properties. The Mgmt2 Properties dialog box appears.
6. Click the Security tab.
7. In the Group Or User Names area, click Authenticated Users.
8. In the Permissions For Authenticated Users selection box, clear Allow Read permission.
9. Click Advanced. An Advanced Security Settings For Mgmt2 dialog box appears.

10. Clear the Allow Inheritable Permissions check box. As shown in the following graphic, a Security message appears.

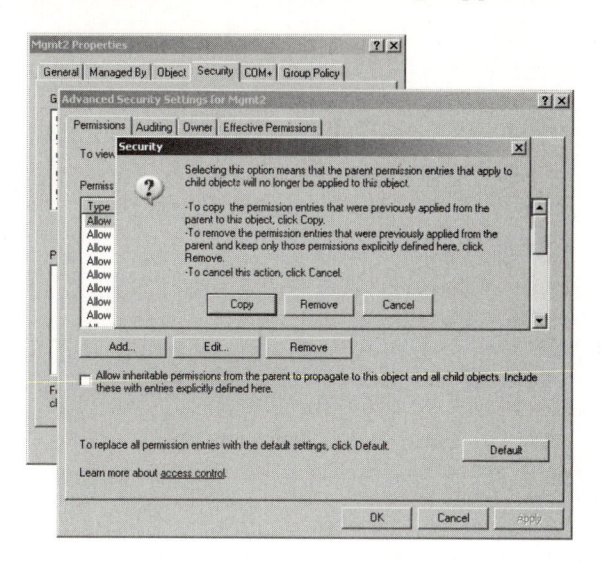

11. Read the message, and click Remove.
12. Click OK in the Advanced Security Settings For Mgmt2 dialog box.
13. Click OK in the Mgmt2 Properties dialog box.
14. Close the Active Directory Users And Computers console.

Finding a User in Active Directory from the Parent Domain

1. On the odd# computer, click Start, and click Search. A Search Results window appears.
2. Expand the Search Results window.
3. In the left window pane, click Other Search Options, click Printers, Computers, Or People, and then click People In Your Address Book. A Find People dialog box appears.
4. In the Look In selection box, ensure Active Directory is selected.
5. Type **User1** in the Name text box, and click Find Now. A Find People warning message appears. Read the message and click OK.

    QUESTION How many users do you find with the username User1?

6. Click Close in the Find People dialog box.
7. Close the Search Results window and log off the computer.

Finding a User in Active Directory from the Child Domain

1. On the even# computer, click Start, and click Search. A Search Results window appears.
2. Expand the Search Results window.
3. In the left window pane, click Other Search Options, click Printers, Computers, Or People, and then click People In Your Address Book. A Find People dialog box appears.
4. In the Look In selection box, ensure that Active Directory is selected.
5. Type **User3** in the Name text box, and click Find Now. A Find People warning message appears. Read the message and click OK.

   QUESTION How many users do you find with the username User3?

6. Click Close in the Find People dialog box.
7. Close the Search Results window and log off the computer.

LAB REVIEW QUESTIONS

Estimated completion time: 15 minutes

1. In your words, describe what you learned during this lab.
2. Which special group allows domain users to search Active Directory by default? What permission does this group have for Active Directory objects by default?
3. If you delegate administrative control over an OU to allow password changes, should that user be able to delete user accounts within the OU?
4. You should not be able to open more than two administrative consoles with the Runas command. True or False?
5. What type of characters can you use in passwords that don't map to the standard keyboard?

LAB CHALLENGE 6-1: USING DSMOVE

Estimated completion time: 10 minutes

Your manager tells you to create three top-level OUs: Acct, AcctPay, and AcctRec. After you do this, your manager tells you to make the AcctRec and AcctPay OUs subordinate to the Acct OU. You decide to accomplish this using the Dsmove program.

Task: Create the three top-level OUs on your local domain. Name them AcctRec, AcctPay, and Acct. Use Dsmove to make the AcctRec and AcctPay OUs subordinate to the Acct OU.

LAB CHALLENGE 6-2: MOVING AN OU WITH MOVETREE

Estimated completion time: 10 minutes

Your manager tells you that the Mgmt1 OU must be moved to a new child domain that was recently added to your company's Active Directory infrastructure.

Task: Move the Mgmt1 OU over from the parent domain to the child domain. (Hint: You must be logged on as a member of the Enterprise Admins group to perform this task.)

LAB CHALLENGE 6-3: MOVING A USER WITH MOVETREE

Estimated completion time: 20 minutes

Your manager wants you to move your user account over to a new domain. You want to verify that the security identifier (SID) changes when you move the user account.

Task: Check the SID of your user account using Whoami /all. Move the user account from one domain to the other. Check the SID of your user account again to verify the SID has changed.

LAB 7
EXPLORING GROUP POLICY ADMINISTRATION

This lab contains the following exercises and activities:

- Exercise 7-1: Configuring the Local Computer Policy
- Exercise 7-2: Processing Order
- Exercise 7-3: Priority Order
- Exercise 7-4: Block Policy Inheritance and No Override
- Exercise 7-5: Using User Group Policy Loopback Processing Mode
- Lab Review Questions
- Lab Challenge 7-1: Disabling the Shutdown Event Tracker
- Lab Challenge 7-2: Hiding Last Logged on User Name

SCENARIO

You are the network administrator of Lucerne Publishing. Lucerne Publishing has offices worldwide. The company has a single Active Directory domain named lucernepublishing.com. The company has 12 locations in 12 different countries: Australia, Egypt, Nigeria, Saudi Arabia, Luxembourg, France, Indonesia, Greece, Germany, Italy, the Netherlands, and the United States of America.

The company network has 15 domain controllers. All of the domain controllers run Microsoft Windows Server 2003, Enterprise Edition. Three domain controllers are located at company headquarters in Tempe, Arizona, USA. The rest of the domain controllers are distributed evenly, one per country, to the company's other locations.

You are employed by the company's United States location and work at the Tempe, Arizona office. Tempe is considered the company headquarters and its network is associated with the American_Site Active Directory site. The other site names are: Au_Site, Egyptian_Site, Nigerian_Site, Saudi_Site, Lux_Site, French_Site, Indo_Site, Greek_Site, German_Site, Italian_Site, and Dutch_Site.

Each country's user and computer accounts are configured in an OU named after the city in which the users and computers are located. The OU names are: Tempe, Melbourne, Cairo, Calabar, Saudi City, Lux City, Paris, Java, Santorini, Berlin, Florence, and Baarn.

You are assigned the task of standardizing the desktops for users across the enterprise. As you gather information about the needs of each location, you realize that you must consider the locale differences and exactly how group policy flows through the domain. You decide to configure your test lab as a single domain with one client, a member server. Then, you decide that you must test the following:

- Domain policy and local computer policy interaction
- Multiple policies and the priority of their application
- Block Policy inheritance versus No Override
- User Group Policy Loopback Processing Mode

After completing this lab, you will be able to:

- Explain how policy inheritance affects the application of Group Policy settings
- Configure some Group Policy Objects (GPOs) to have a higher priority than other GPOs
- Configure OUs with Block Policy inheritance
- Enable No Override on GPOs
- Configure User Group Policy Loopback Processing Mode

Estimated lesson time: 170 minutes

> **NOTE** In this lab, you will see the characters **xx**, **yy**, and **zz**. These directions assume that you are working on computers configured in pairs and that each computer has a number. One number is odd and the other number is even. For example, Computer01 is the odd# computer and Computer02 is the even# computer. When you see **xx**, substitute the unique number assigned to the odd# computer. When you see **yy**, substitute the unique number assigned to the even# computer. When you see **zz**, substitute the number assigned to the computer you are working at, either odd or even.
>
> Whenever you see the Manage Your Server page appear in this lab, select the Don't Display This Page At Logon check box and close the Manage Your Server page.

LAB DEPENDENCIES

In order to complete this lab, you must be sure that the following is done:

- The even# computer must be configured to use the odd# computer as its Preferred DNS Server, as explained in Exercise 1-4.
- Active Directory is installed on the odd# computer. Exercise 2-1 covers the installation of Active Directory on the odd# computer.
- Active Directory is installed on the even# computer. Exercises 2-3 and 2-4 cover the installation of Active Directory on the even# computer.
- Users have the right to log on to domain controllers. Exercise 4-1 explains how to complete this configuration.

EXERCISE 7-1: CONFIGURING THE LOCAL COMPUTER POLICY

Estimated completion time: 35 minutes

You need to prepare your test lab for your upcoming experiments. First, you must demote a child domain you have configured. Then, you must configure your member server as a domain member. Finally, you want to test the implementation of a Local Computer Policy before you move on to testing Group Policy Objects (GPOs).

To demote the child domain controller and re-join the parent domain:

1. On the even# computer, log on as the default administrator on the child*xx* domain.

2. Open a command prompt and type **dcpromo /Answer:"C:\Lab Manual\Lab07\RemoveChild*xx*.txt"**. Press ENTER. After your child domain controller is demoted, your computer is automatically restarted.

3. Log on to the even# computer as the default administrator of the local computer.

4. Join the even# computer to the domain*xx*.local domain (Lab 2, Exercise 2-3).

Configure the even# computer to remove the Run menu from the Start menu

1. Log on to the even# computer as the default administrator of the local computer.

2. Open the Run dialog box. Type **gpedit.msc** and click OK. The Group Policy Object Editor opens the Local Computer Policy.

3. Under the User Configuration object, expand the Administrative Templates object.

4. Click the Start Menu And Taskbar object.

5. In the right window pane, double-click the Remove Run Menu From Start Menu setting. The Remove Run Menu From Start Menu Properties dialog box appears.

6. Select the Enabled radio button as shown in the following figure. Click OK.

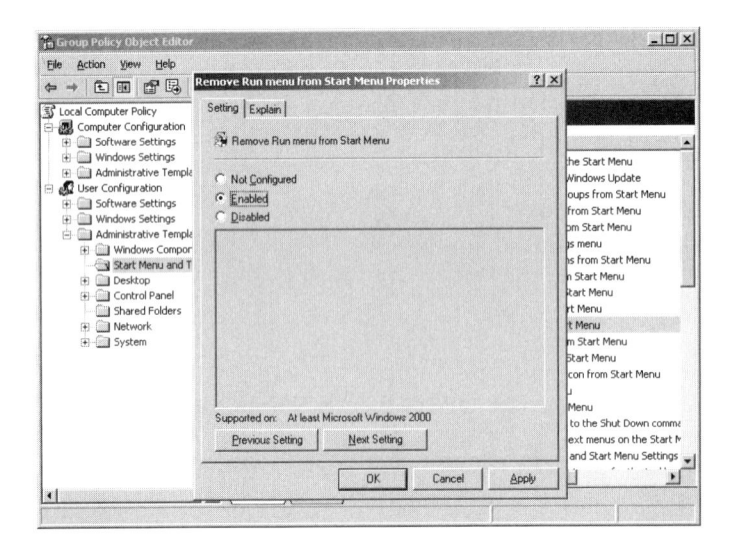

7. Close the Group Policy Object Editor.

8. Log off and then log on again as the default administrator of the local computer. This will update the Group Policy for this user account.

9. Click the Start button on the taskbar.

   QUESTION Do you see the Run menu in the Start menu? Explain this result.

EXERCISE 7-2: PROCESSING ORDER

Estimated completion time: 30 minutes

The administrators in Calabar and Cairo are concerned with the potential implementation of domain-wide policies. Specifically, they are concerned about domain policies overriding configured computer settings. You want to find out if they are correct.

Configure the Remove Run Policy Setting on the Domain

1. On the odd# computer, log on as the default administrator of the domain*xx* domain.

2. Open Active Directory Users And Computers. Right-click the domain*xx*.local object and then click Properties.

3. Click the Group Policy tab. As shown in the figure below, The Default Domain Policy should be selected.

[Screenshot: domain01.local Properties dialog, Group Policy tab, showing Default Domain Policy]

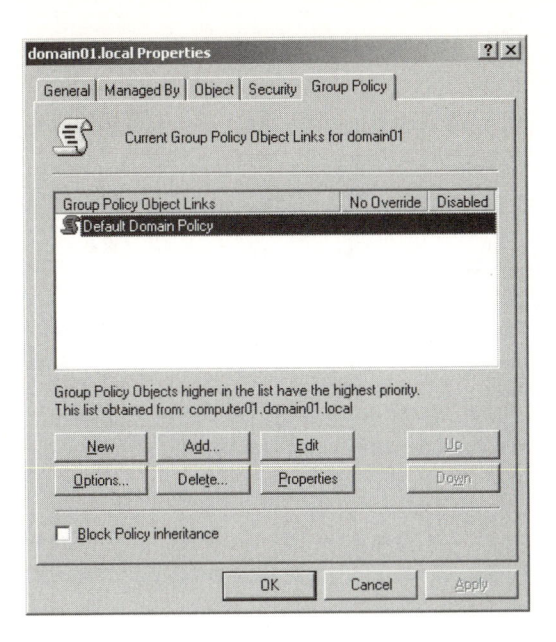

4. Click Edit. The Group Policy Object Editor opens the Default Domain Policy.

5. Under the User Configuration object, expand the Administrative Templates object.

6. Click the Start Menu And Taskbar object.

7. In the right window pane, double-click the Remove Run Menu From Start Menu setting. The Remove Run Menu From Start Menu Properties dialog box appears.

8. Select the Disabled radio button. Click OK.

9. Close the Group Policy Object Editor and the domain*xx*.local Properties dialog box.

Verify Domain GPO Overrides Local Computer Policy

1. On the even# computer, log off and then log on as the default administrator of the domain*xx* domain.

    This will update the Group Policy for this user account.

2. Click the Start button on the taskbar.

    QUESTION Do you see the Run menu in the Start menu?

    QUESTION Based on the results, how is Group Policy processed?

Creating users for testing

1. On the odd# computer, open the Active Directory Users And Computers console.

LAB 7: EXPLORING GROUP POLICY ADMINISTRATION

2. Create a user account named **L7DomUser** in the Users container of domain*xx*.local. (Reference Lab Exercise 4-1).

3. Create a new top-level OU named **L7Test1** in domain*xx*.local (Reference Lab Exercise 6-3).

4. Create a user account in the L7Test1 OU named **L7Test1User**.

Creating GPO Links on the Domain

1. On the odd# computer, open the Active Directory Users And Computers console.

2. In the left window pane, right-click the domain*xx*.local domain. Click Properties. The domain*xx*.local Properties dialog box appears.

3. Click the Group Policy tab.

4. Click New. A New Group Policy Object appears under the Group Policy Object Links.

5. Rename the policy **RemoveHelp1** and press ENTER.

6. Click Edit. The Group Policy Object Editor opens the RemoveHelp1 GPO.

7. Under the User Configuration object, expand the Administrative Templates object in the left window pane.

8. Click the Start Menu And Taskbar object.

9. In the right window pane, double-click the Remove Help Menu From Start Menu setting. The Remove Help Menu From Start Menu Properties dialog box appears.

10. Select the Enabled radio button. Click OK.

11. Close the Group Policy Object editor.

12. In the domain*xx*.local Properties dialog box, click New. The New Group Policy Object appears under the Group Policy Object Links.

13. Rename the policy **RemoveSearch1** and press ENTER.

14. Use the technique you used in the previous steps to Enable the Remove Search Menu From Start Menu setting in the RemoveSearch1 GPO. Close the Group Policy Object Editor and domain*xx*.local Properties dialog box when you are finished.

Creating GPO Links on the OU

1. On the odd# computer, in the left window pane of Active Directory Users And Computers, expand the domain*xx*.local object. Then right click the L7Test1 OU and click Properties.

2. Click the Group Policy tab.

3. Click New. The New Group Policy object appears under the Group Policy Object Links.

4. Rename the policy **AddHelp1** and press ENTER.

5. Use the technique you used in the previous section to Disable the Remove Help Menu From Start Menu setting in the AddHelp1 GPO. Close the Group Policy Object Editor when you are done.

6. Create another GPO linked to the L7Test1 OU named **RemoveRun2**. Enable the Remove Run Menu From Start Menu setting in the RemoveRun2 GPO.

7. Close the Group Policy Object Editor and click Close in the L7Test1 Properties dialog box.

8. Close Active Directory Users And Computers.

Testing the Results

1. On the even# computer, log on as L7DomUser of the domain*xx* domain.

2. Click the Start button on the taskbar.

   QUESTION Do you see a Search menu option?

   QUESTION Do you see a Help And Support menu option?

   QUESTION Do you see a Run menu option?

3. Log off and then log on as the L7Test1User of the domain*xx* domain.

   QUESTION Do you see a Search menu option?

   QUESTION Do you see a Help And Support menu option?

   QUESTION Do you see a Run menu option?

   QUESTION Why are there differences between what these user accounts see in the Start menu?

EXERCISE 7-3: PRIORITY ORDER

Estimated completion time: 10 minutes

Administrators in Baarn tell you that they have several subordinate OUs. They want to know what happens when they link two conflicting policies on the same OU.

Another GPO for L7Test1

NOTE During this exercise, you will be switching from the odd# computer to the even# computer and vice versa. When you switch from one computer to another computer, it is important that you remain on that computer for the steps that follow until asked to switch again.

1. On the odd# computer, create a new GPO named **AddRun1** (Reference Lab Exercise 7-2) and linked to the L7Test1 OU.

2. Edit the AddRun1 GPO and configure the Remove Run Menu From Start Menu setting to be Disabled (Reference Lab Exercise 7-2).

3. On the even# computer, log off and log on as L7Test1User of the domain*xx* domain.

    QUESTION Can you see the Run menu option on the Start menu?

    QUESTION Why did the AddRun1 GPO link not add the Run menu option to the Start menu?

4. On the odd# computer, open the L7Test1 OU Properties dialog box from within the Active Directory Users And Computers console, and click the Group Policy tab.

5. Click the AddRun1 GPO link and then click Up twice. Ensure that the AddRun1 GPO link is at the top of the Group Policy Object Links column as shown in the following figure.

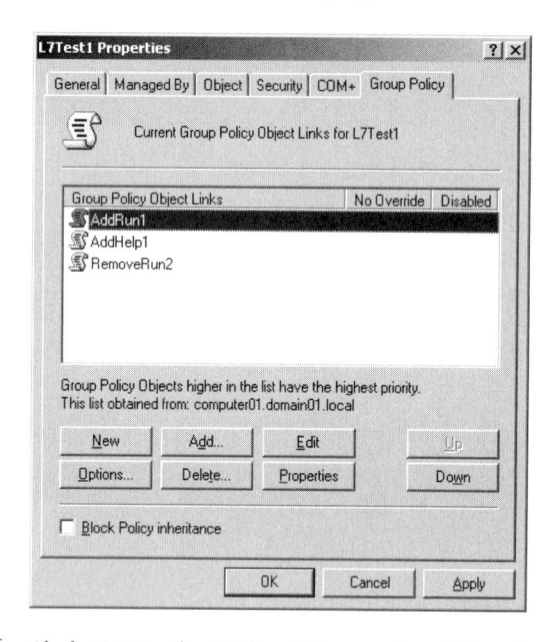

6. Click OK in the L7Test1 Properties dialog box.

7. On the even# computer, open a command prompt window. Click Start, click All Programs, click Accessories, and then click Command Prompt.

8. In the Command Prompt window, type **gpupdate**, and press ENTER.

9. Click the Start button on the taskbar.

    QUESTION Can you see the Run menu option on the Start menu?

    QUESTION Why did the AddRun1 GPO link add the Run menu option to the Start menu?

EXERCISE 7-4: BLOCK POLICY INHERITANCE AND NO OVERRIDE

Estimated completion time: 25 minutes

It is not necessary that all GPO settings apply to all users or computers in the domain. Some users and computers do not need parts of the configuration. You want to be able to control what settings transfer down from the domain to specific OUs.

> **NOTE** During this exercise, you will switch from the odd# computer to the even# computer, and vice versa. When you switch from one computer to another computer, you must remain on that computer for the steps that follow until asked to switch again.

1. On the odd# computer, open the L7Test1 OU Properties dialog box from within the Active Directory Users And Computers console and click the Group Policy tab.

2. Select one of the GPO links and click Delete. The Delete dialog box appears.

3. Select the Remove The Link And Delete The Group Policy Object Permanently radio button and click OK. The Delete Group Policy Object message box appears.

4. Click Yes.

5. Repeat steps 2–4 until there are no GPO links listed.

6. Click Close.

7. On the even# computer, type **gpupdate** at the command prompt, and press ENTER.

8. Click the Start button on the taskbar.

   QUESTION Do you see a Search menu option? Explain this result.

   QUESTION Do you see a Help And Support menu option? Explain this result.

   QUESTION Do you see a Run menu option? Explain this result.

9. On the odd# computer, open the L7Test1 Properties dialog box from within the Active Directory Users And Computers console and click the Group Policy tab.

10. Select the Block Policy Inheritance check box to enable inheritance blocking.

11. Click OK in the L7Test1 Properties dialog box.

12. On the even# computer, type **gpupdate** at the command prompt, and press ENTER.

13. Click the Start button on the taskbar.

    QUESTION   Do you see a Search menu option? Explain this result.

    QUESTION   Do you see a Help And Support menu option? Explain this result.

    QUESTION   Do you see a Run menu option? Explain this result.

14. On the odd# computer, open the domain*xx*.local domain Properties dialog box from within the Active Directory Users And Computers console and click the Group Policy tab.

15. The Default Domain Policy should be selected. Click Options. The Default Domain Policy Options dialog box appears.

16. Select the No Override: Prevents Other Group Policy Objects From Overriding Policy Set In This One check box and click OK, as shown in the figure below.

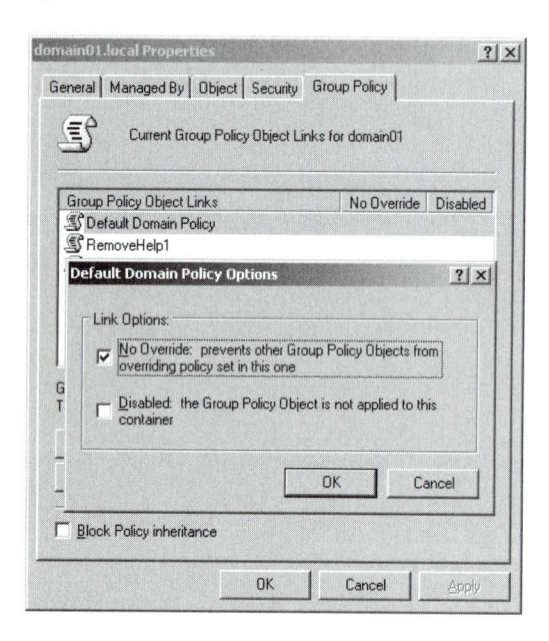

17. Click OK on the domain*xx*.local Properties dialog box.

18. On the even# computer, type **gpupdate** at the command prompt, and press ENTER.

19. Click the Start button on the taskbar.

    QUESTION   Do you see a Search menu option? Explain this result.

    QUESTION   Do you see a Help And Support menu option? Explain this result.

    QUESTION   Do you see a Run menu option? Explain this result.

EXERCISE 7-5: USING USER GROUP POLICY LOOPBACK PROCESSING MODE

Estimated completion time: 20 minutes

Each top-level OU in your company has a single subordinate OU named EmployeeAccess. Each of these OUs contains two computers that users visiting from other countries can use. These systems are a concern for all administrators because administrators want visiting users to be subject to stricter controls than employees of that location. You need to set up a method for securing these EmployeeAccess computers so that visiting user desktops are locked down.

> **NOTE** During this exercise, you will be switching from the odd# computer to the even# computer and vice versa. When you switch from one computer to another computer, it is important that you remain on that computer for the steps that follow until asked to switch again.

1. On the odd# computer, create a new top-level OU named **L7Test2** in domain*xx*.local (Reference Lab Exercise 6-3).

2. In the left window of Active Directory Users And Computers, click the Computers container.

3. In the right window pane, right-click computer*yy* and click Move. The Move dialog box appears.

4. Select the L7Test2 OU object and then click OK as shown in the figure below.

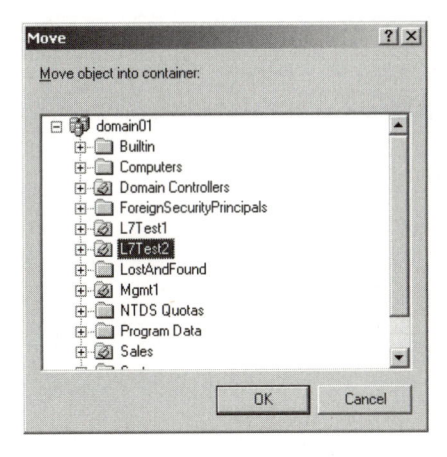

5. Open the L7Test2 Properties dialog box from within the Active Directory Users And Computers console and click the Group Policy tab.

6. Create a new GPO named **DisableCP** linked to the L7Test2 OU.

7. Edit the DisableCP GPO and configure the Prohibit Access To The Control Panel setting to Enabled.

> **NOTE** This setting can be found under User Configuration, Administrative Templates, and Control Panel in the GPO editor.

8. On the even# computer, log off and log on as L7DomUser of the domain*xx* domain.

9. Click Start and then click Control Panel.

    QUESTION Why are you able to access Control Panel using L7DomUser credentials?

10. On the odd# computer, edit the DisableCP GPO and configure the User Group Policy Loopback Processing Mode setting to Enabled.

    NOTE This setting can be found under Computer Configuration, Administrative Templates, System, and Group Policy in the GPO editor. Leave the Mode setting configured for Replace.

11. Configure the Remove Run Menu From Start Menu setting to Enabled.

12. Configure the Remove Search Menu From Start Menu setting to Disabled.

13. Close the Group Policy Object Editor.

14. Click OK on the L7Test2 Properties dialog box.

15. On the even# computer, open a command prompt as an administrator and run Gpupdate. Follow these steps. Type **runas /user:administrator@domain*xx*.local "cmd"** into the Run dialog box or a command prompt window and press ENTER. Type the administrator password when prompted and then type **gpupdate** in the opened command prompt window. Press ENTER to complete the process.

    NOTE User Group Policy Loopback Processing Mode is a computer setting. You need to run Gpupdate as an administrator.

16. On the even# computer, log off and log on as L7DomUser.

17. Click the Start button on the taskbar.

    QUESTION Do you see a Search menu option?

    QUESTION Why does the Search menu option appear in the Start menu now?

    QUESTION Do you see a Run menu option?

    QUESTION Why does the Run menu option appear in the Start menu now?

    QUESTION Are you able to access Control Panel? Explain your results.

LAB REVIEW QUESTIONS

Estimated completion time: 15 minutes

1. In your words, describe what you learned during this lab.

2. Conflicts between the Local Computer Policy and the GPOs linked to the domain are always won by which policy setting?

3. If there are multiple policies configured at the domain, and you only want one of those policies to flow down to a given OU, what should you do to the OU? What should you do to the policy that you want to flow down?

4. You have two conflicting policies, PolicyA and PolicyB. Each is linked to the same OU named Marketing. PolicyA settings are implemented over PolicyB settings, but you need PolicyB settings to be implemented instead of PolicyA settings. You do not want to use No Override because that affects all subordinate OUs. What should you do?

5. The No Override setting on a GPO overrides which two policy control measures?

LAB CHALLENGE 7-1: DISABLING THE SHUTDOWN EVENT TRACKER

Estimated completion time: 15 minutes

You want to disable the Shutdown Event Tracker so that you do not have to select a reason for turning off your test computers.

- You must create a Group Policy named DSET and link the GPO to the domain. Set the Display Shutdown Event Tracker setting to Disabled.

LAB CHALLENGE 7-2: HIDING LAST LOGGED ON USER NAME

Estimated completion time: 15 minutes

The network administrators in Saudi Arabia do not like that the last logged on user name is displayed in the Welcome To Windows dialog box. They do not want network users to be able to find out other network users' user names so easily.

- You must Create a group policy named ClearName1 and link the GPO to the domain. Set the Interactive Logon: Do Not Display Last User Name setting to Disabled.

POST-LAB CLEANUP

Estimated completion time: 5 minutes

1. Permanently delete all new GPO objects that you created in this Lab (Reference Lab Exercise 7-4). Do not delete the Default Domain Policy. Delete the following GPOs, if they are linked to domain*xx*.local:
    - ClearName1
    - DSET
    - RemoveHelp1
    - RemoveSearch1

2. Move the even# computer account from the L7Test2 OU to the Computers container (Reference Lab Exercise 7-5).

3. Delete the two OUs created in this lab:
   - ❑ L7Test1
   - ❑ L7Test2

4. Edit the Default Domain Policy and set the Remove Run Menu From Start Menu setting to Not Configured (Reference Lab Exercise 7-1).

5. For Default Domain Policy, clear the No Override option (Reference Lab Exercise 7-4).

6. On the even# computer, edit the Local Computer Policy and set the Remove Run Menu From Start Menu setting to Not Configured (Reference Lab Exercise 7-1). (To run Local Computer Policy, type **gpedit.msc** at a command prompt.)

7. Run Gpupdate to refresh group policy settings.

8. Log off and log on as default administrator. Ensure the Help And Support, Search, and Run menus are listed on the Start menu. If not, try restarting or verifying the Post-Lab Cleanup steps.

LAB 8
MANAGING USERS AND COMPUTERS WITH GROUP POLICY

This lab contains the following exercises and activities:

- Exercise 8-1: Account Policies
- Exercise 8-2: Audit Policies
- Exercise 8-3: Folder Redirection
- Exercise 8-4: Disk Quotas
- Lab Review Questions
- Lab Challenge 8-1: Managing the Password Policy
- Lab Challenge 8-2: Configuring the Account Lockout Policy

SCENARIO

You are a network administrator for Fabrikam. Fabrikam uses a single Active Directory domain. There are three Windows Server 2003 domain controllers and 500 client computers running Windows XP Professional on the network.

Recently, a security consulting company conducted an analysis of the network. Your manager wants you to address the following issues:

- Password cracking software was run on the network and target accounts were never locked out.
- Files identified by management as confidential files are not monitored.
- Passwords shorter than some departments require are used on the network.

Your manager wants you to back up the My Documents folders of all Marketing Department users each day. You are concerned that this may lead to a shortage of disk space on the server. You also want to ensure that users' disk space is limited on any file server to which they might save files.

After completing this lab, you will be able to:

- Enforce a Password Policy
- Administer an Account Lockout Policy
- Configure security auditing
- Redirect users' folders to a central location
- Enable centralized disk quotas

Estimated lesson time: 150 minutes

> **NOTE** In this lab, you will see the characters xx, yy, and zz. These directions assume that you are working on computers configured in pairs and that each computer has a number. One number is odd and the other number is even. For example, Computer01 is the odd# computer, and Computer02 is the even# computer. When you see xx, substitute the unique number assigned to the odd# computer. When you see yy, substitute the unique number assigned to the even# computer. When you see zz, substitute the number assigned to the computer you are working at, either odd or even.
>
> Whenever you see the Manage Your Servers page appear in this lab, select the Don't Display This Page At Logon check box and close the Manage Your Server page.

LAB DEPENDENCIES

In order to complete this lab, you must be sure that the following is done:

- The even# computer must be configured to use the odd# computer as its Preferred DNS Server, as explained in Lab Exercise 1-4.
- Active Directory is installed on the odd# computer. Lab Exercise 2-1 covers the installation of Active Directory on the odd# computer.
- Users have the right to log on to domain controllers. Lab Exercise 4-1 explains how to complete this configuration.
- The even# computer must be a member of the odd# computer's domain, as shown in Lab Exercise 2-3.
- The even# computer must not be a domain controller for the child domain. If the even# computer is a domain controller for the child domain, you must demote it as shown in Lab Exercise 7-1.

EXERCISE 8-1: ACCOUNT POLICIES

Estimated completion time: 20 minutes

Some departments in your company require a 14-character password on user accounts. You want to ensure that users are required to use 14-character passwords. Furthermore, you need to address the issue that the security consultants identified concerning account lockout. The security consultants were able to run a password cracker on your network without locking out a single user account. You want to ensure that anyone who is trying to guess a user account by trying different passwords is locked out.

NOTE During this exercise you will be switching from the odd# computer to the even# computer and vice versa. When you switch from one computer to another computer, it is important that you remain on that computer for the steps that follow until asked to switch again.

To adjust the Password Policy:

1. On the odd# computer, log on as the default administrator of the domain*xx* domain.
2. If you do not already have one, create an organizational unit (OU) named Marketing (Reference Lab Exercise 6-3).
3. Create and link a new GPO to the Marketing OU named PwdPol1 (Reference Lab Exercise 7-2).
4. Edit the PwdPol1 GPO (Reference Lab Exercise 7-2).
5. In the left window pane of the Group Policy Object Editor, under the Computer Configuration object, expand the following objects: Windows Settings, Security Settings, and Account Policies.
6. Click on the Password Policy object.
7. Double-click the Minimum Password Length setting to open the Minimum Password Length Properties box.
8. Select the Define This Policy Setting check box. Configure the Characters selection box to read Password Must Be At Least 14 Characters. Click OK.

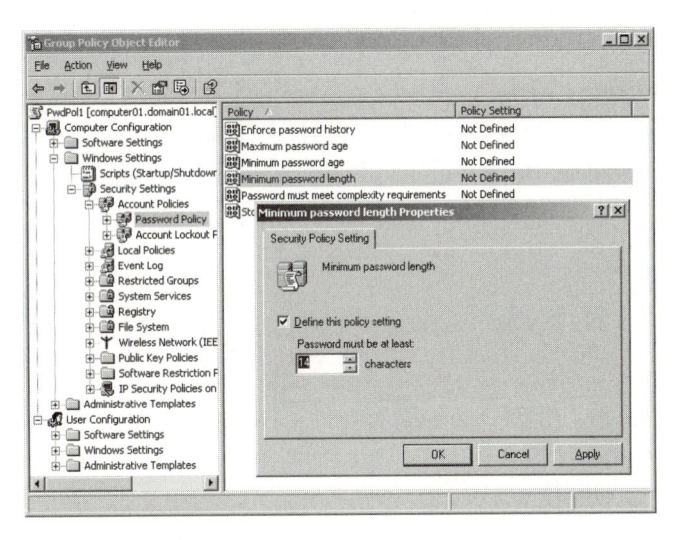

9. Close the Group Policy Object Editor and the Marketing Properties dialog box.
10. Create a user account named Lab8User1 in the Marketing OU with a password of **MSPress#1** and clear the User Must Change Password At Next Logon check box.

    QUESTION MSPress#1 is only a nine-character password. Why do you not have to use a 14-character password?

11. Open the domain*xx*.local Properties dialog box from within the Active Directory Users And Computers console, and click the Group Policy tab (Reference Lab Exercise 7.2).

12. Click Add. The Add A Group Policy Object Link dialog box appears.

13. Click the All tab and then click the Group Policy Object named PwdPol1 shown in the All Group Policy Objects Stored In The Domain list. (See the following figure.)

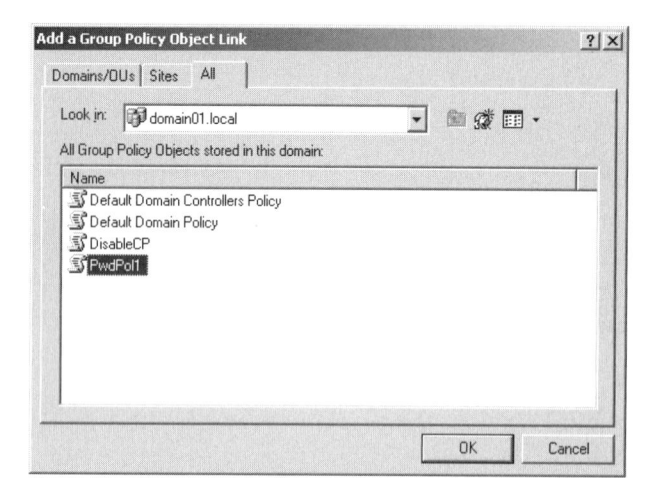

14. Click OK.

15. Select and move the PwdPol1 link so that it is above the Default Domain Policy by using the Up button.

16. Click OK in the domain*xx*.local Properties dialog box.

17. Remove the GPO link named PwdPol1 from the Marketing OU. Open the Marketing Properties dialog box and click the Group Policy tab.

18. Click PwdPol1 in Group Policy Object Links and click Delete as shown in the following figure.

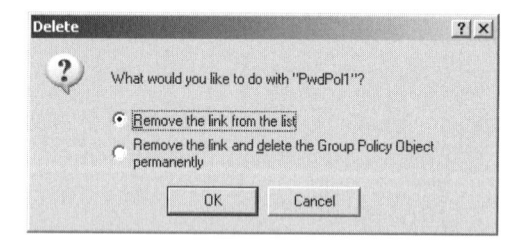

19. Click the Remove The Link From The List radio button and click OK.

    NOTE *Do not click the Remove The Link And Delete The Group Policy Object Permanently radio button.*

20. Select the Block Policy Inheritance check box on the Marketing OU (Reference Lab Exercise 7-4). Click OK in the Marketing Properties dialog box.

21. On the even# computer, log on as Lab8User1 on the domain*xx* domain.

    QUESTION *Are you able to log on with a password that is less than 14 characters?*

22. Open a command prompt window, type **gpupdate**, and press ENTER.
23. On the odd# computer, create a user account in the Marketing OU named Lab8User2 and try to configure the password as MSPress#1. An Active Directory message box appears. Read the message and click OK.

    QUESTION What happened after you clicked Finish?

24. Click Back.
25. Type **MSPress#1MSPress#1** into the Password text box and the Confirm Password text box.
26. Click Next and then click Finish.

    QUESTION Does this password work?

    QUESTION What did you learn about Password Policy inheritance?

Adjusting the Account Lockout Policy:

1. Use the technique you learned in the previous section to edit the PwdPol1 GPO. Configure the Account Lockout Threshold setting for 3 Invalid Logon Attempts. When you click OK to configure this setting, a Suggested Value Changes message box appears. Click OK.

    NOTE The Account Lockout Threshold setting can be found under Computer Configuration, Windows Settings, Security Settings, Account Policies, Account Lockout Policy in the Group Policy Object Editor.

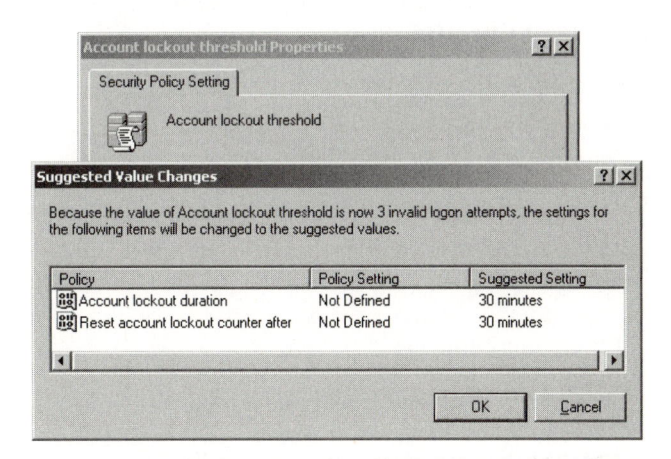

2. Close the Group Plicy Object Editor and close the domain*xx*.local Perperties dialog box.
3. On the even# computer, log off and attempt to log on with the Lab8User1 credentials, but when providing the password credentials, use the password **MSP**. Repeat this process three more times.

    QUESTION What happens to the Lab8User1 account?

4. Attempt to log on using the correct password of **MSPress#1**.

5. On the odd# computer, unlock the user account. Open the Active Directory Users And Computers console and click the Marketing OU in the left console pane. Right-click Lab8User1 and click Properties. The Lab1User Properties dialog box appears as shown in the following figure. Click the Account tab and then clear the Account Is Locked Out check box. Click OK.

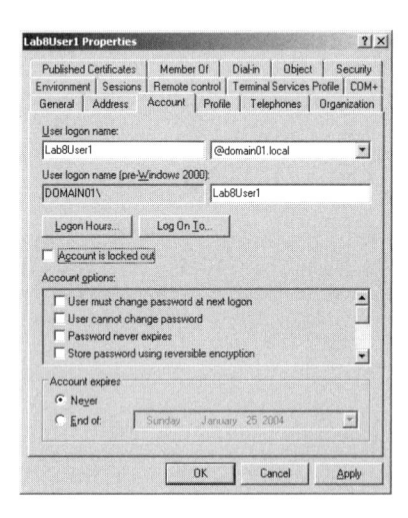

6. On the even# computer, verify that you can log on as Lab8User1 with the password MSPress#1. Log off.

EXERCISE 8-2: AUDIT POLICIES

Estimated completion time: 30 minutes

The security consultants found that confidential files were not monitored for hacking attempts. You want to configure auditing of all confidential files.

> **NOTE** This exercise can be done on either of the computers. When you perform this exercise on the odd# computer, you will be working with the domain. When working on the even# computer, you can open Gpedit.msc from the Run dialog box to modify the Local Computer Policy.

To configure auditing of all confidential files:

1. Log on as the default administrator of the domain.xx domain.

2. Create a new folder named ConfidentialFiles on the C: drive.

3. Right-click the folder named ConfidentialFiles and click Properties. The ConfidentialFiles Properties dialog box appears.

4. Click the Security tab and then click Advanced. The Advanced Security Settings For ConfidentialFiles dialog box appears.

5. Click the Auditing tab and then click Add. The Select User, Computer Or Group dialog box appears.

6. Type **Everyone** in the Enter Object Name To Select text box and click Check Names. Verify that Everyone is underlined and click OK. The Auditing Entry For ConfidentialFiles dialog box appears.

7. In the Access box select both the Successful and Failed check boxes for the List Folder/Read Data access type as shown in the following figure.

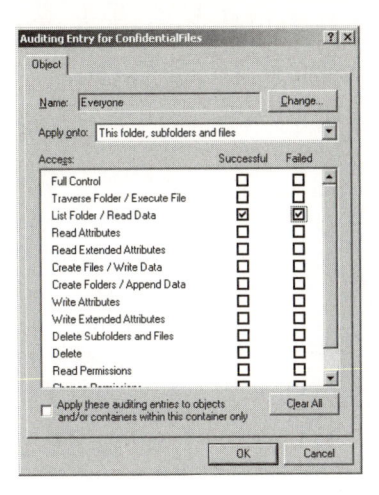

8. Click OK.

9. Click OK in the Advanced Security Settings For ConfidentialFiles dialog box.

10. Click OK in the ConfidentialFiles Properties dialog box.

11. Create two text files in the ConfidentialFiles folder. Name one file Confidential1.txt and the other Confidential2.txt. Enter the text **Lab8 auditing test** in each file.

12. Click Start and then click Run.

13. Type **eventvwr.msc** in the Open box. Click OK.

14. Expand the Event Viewer if necessary.

15. Click Security in the left console pane.

16. Scroll down in the right details pane and you should not see any audit events recorded here yet. You must first enable Audit Object Access.

17. If you are performing this exercise on the odd# computer, create a new GPO named Audit1, and link it to the Domain Controllers OU. If you are performing this exercise on the even# computer, edit the Local Security Policy instead of creating a GPO named Audit1.

18. Edit the Audit1 GPO (on the odd# computer) or the Local Computer Policy (on the even# computer). Under the Computer Configuration object in the left window pane, expand the following objects: Windows Settings, Security SEttings, and Local Policies.

19. In the left window pane, click the Audit Policy object. In the right window pane double-click the Audit Object Access setting. The Audit Object Access Properties box opens.

20. On the odd# computer, select the Define These Policy Settings check box. On both computers, select the Success and Failure check boxes. Click OK.

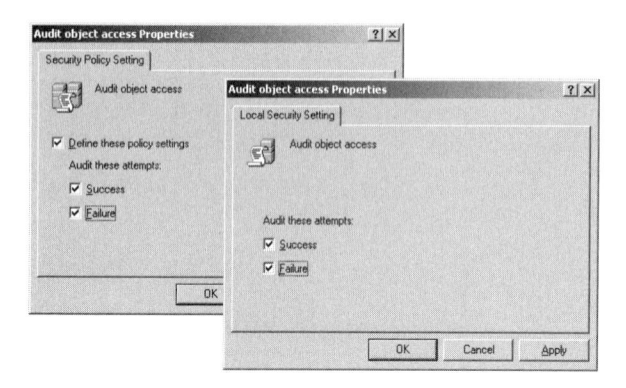

21. Close the Group Policy Object Editor.

22. If you are performing this exercise on the odd# computer, give the Audit1GPO a higher priority than the Default Domain Controllers Policy (Reference Lab Exercise 7-3). Click Close in the Domain Controllers Properties dialog box.

23. Close all open windows, log off and log on as Lab8User1 on the domain*xx* domain.

24. Open the folder named ConfidentialFiles, open the file named Confidential1.txt, and then close the file.

25. Log off and log on as Lab8User2 on the domain*xx* domain. Remember, the password is MSPress#1MSPress#1.

26. Open the folder named ConfidentialFiles, open the file named Confidential2.txt, and then close the file.

27. Open a command prompt window.

28. Type **runas /user:administrator@domain.*xx*.local "mmc eventvwr.msc"** into the command prompt window and press ENTER. Enter the password for the administrator and press ENTER.

29. Click the Security log in the left console pane.

30. In the right window pane, look for Object Access events from Lab8User1 or Lab8User2 that have Event ID 560. When you find one, double-click it. The Event Properties dialog box opens as shown in the following figure.

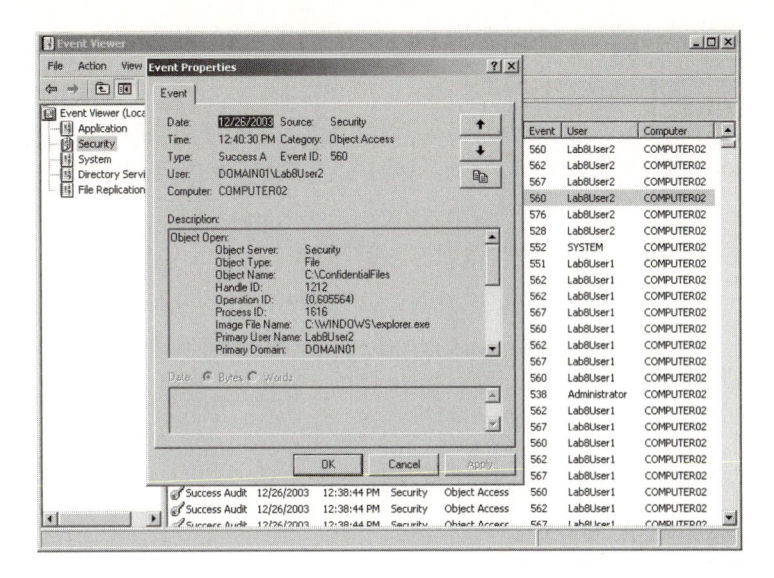

QUESTION Does the Security log tell you which folder and files have been accessed?

QUESTION Does the Security log tell you who tried to access the files?

QUESTION Does the security log tell you if the access attempt succeeded or failed?

31. Close all open windows and log off.

EXERCISE 8-3: FOLDER REDIRECTION

Estimated completion time: 15 minutes

Many of the production users in your company have important files stored in their My Documents folders. You want to redirect all of the mobile users' documents to a central location to facilitate backup.

NOTE During this exercise, you will be switching from the odd# computer to the even# computer and vice versa. When you switch from one computer to another computer it is important that you remain on that computer for the steps that follow until asked to switch again.

To redirect documents to a central location:

1. On the odd# computer, log on as the default administrator of the domain*xx* domain.
2. Create a folder named Lab8MyDocs1 on the C: drive.
3. Share the Lab8MyDocs1 folder to the Everyone group. Allow the Everyone group Full Control access to this share.

4. Create and link a new GPO named Redirect1 to the Marketing OU.

5. Click Edit to edit the Redirect1 GPO.

6. In the left window pane, under the User Configuration object, expand the Windows Settings object, and then click on the Folder Redirection object.

7. In the right window pane, right-click My Documents and click Properties. The My Documents Properties dialog box appears.

8. In the Setting selection box, select the Basic option.

9. Ensure that the Target Folder Location reads: Create A Folder For Each User Under The Root Path. Type **\\Computer*xx*\Lab8MyDocs1** into the Root Path text box and click OK as shown in the following figure.

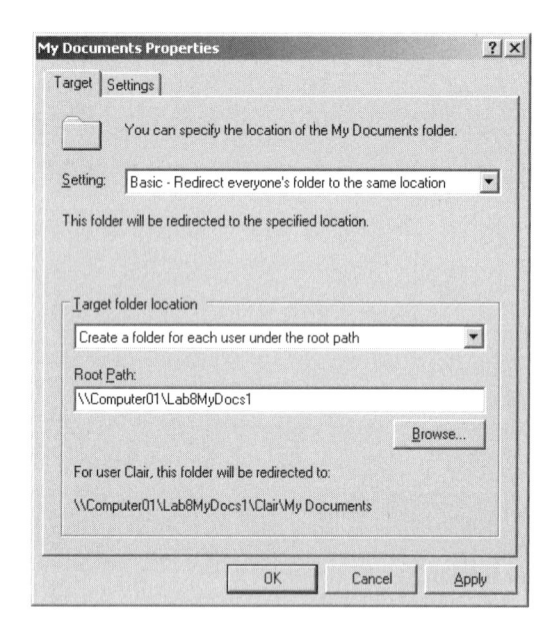

10. Close the Group Policy Object Editor and close the Marketing Properties dialog box.

11. On the even# computer, log on as Lab8User1 on the domain*xx* domain.

12. On the odd# computer, open the Lab8MyDocs1 folder.

    QUESTION Do you see a folder named Lab8User1?

13. Open the Lab8User1 folder.

    QUESTION Is the My Documents folder for Lab8User1 redirected?

14. Log off the even# computer.

EXERCISE 8-4: DISK QUOTAS

Estimated completion time: 30 minutes

You are concerned that users are saving too much data to the servers on your network. You want to try enabling disk quotas to see if this is a possible solution for that problem.

To enable disk quotas:

1. On the odd# computer, create and link a new GPO named DiskQuota1 to the domain*xx*.local domain (Reference Lab Exercise 7-2).
2. Click Edit to edit the DiskQuota1 GPO.
3. In the left window pane, under the Computer Configuration object, expand Administrative Templates, expand System, and then click on the Disk Quotas object.
4. In the right window pane, double-click Enable Disk Quotas. The Enable Disk Quotas Properties dialog box appears.
5. Select the Enabled radio button.
6. Click Next Setting. The Enforce Disk Quota Limit Properties dialog box appears.
7. Select the Enabled radio button.
8. Click Next Setting. The Default Quota Limit And Warning Level Properties dialog box appears.
9. Select the Enabled radio button.
10. Set the Default Quota Limit Value box to 1. Ensure the Units box remains set to MB.
11. Scroll down the window until you can see the Default Warning Level settings.
12. Set the Default Warning Level Value to 512.

    CAUTION *The size of a user profile can vary depending on hard disk and sector size. If you experience difficulties logging on after making this change, you may need to increase the quota size.*

13. Set the units to KB.

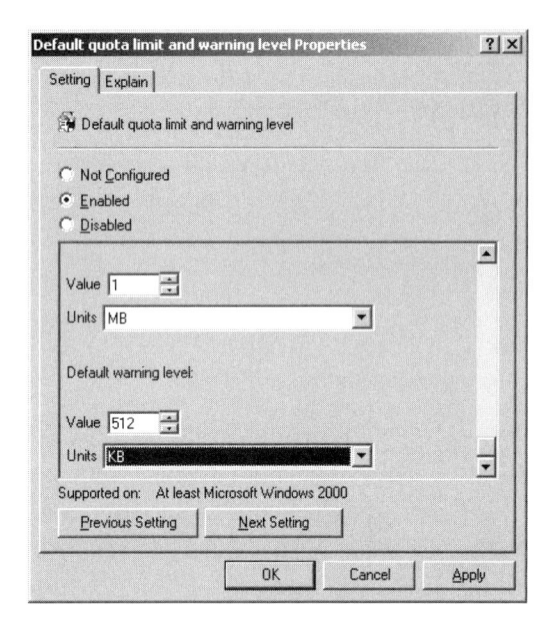

LAB 8: MANAGING USERS AND COMPUTERS WITH GROUP POLICY

14. Click OK.

15. Close the Group Policy Object Editor, and close the domain*xx*.local Properties dialog box.

16. Create a new user account named Lab8User3 in the Marketing OU, set the password to MSPress#MSPress#1, and clear the User Must Change Password At Next Logon check box.

17. Close Active Directory Users And Computers.

18. Restart both computers, first the odd# computer, and then the even# computer.

19. On the even# computer, log on as Lab8User3 on the domain*xx* domain.

20. Create a new bitmap image. Right-click the Desktop in an area without any icons, click New, and click Bitmap Image.

21. Type **Lab8Test.bmp** and press ENTER to rename the file.

22. Press the Print Screen key to take a screen capture of your Desktop.

23. Right-click the file named Lab8Test.bmp and click Edit. The file is opened with Paint, a Windows accessory program.

24. Click the Edit menu and then click Paste.

25. Click the File menu and then click Save.

26. Read the Paint message box that appears.

    QUESTION Why does this error occur?

27. Click OK.

28. Close Paint and don't save the changes.

29. On the even# computer, log off.

30. Log on to the even# computer using the following user accounts in sequence: Lab8User1, Lab8User2, and the default administrator of the domain*xx* domain. Each time you log on, attempt the experiment of creating and saving a bitmap.

    QUESTION Did any of your attempts to create and save a bitmap work?

LAB REVIEW QUESTIONS

Estimated completion time: 15 minutes

1. In your words, describe what you learned during this lab.
2. When you create a GPO to implement a new Password Policy, where must you link the GPO in order to have the policy take affect?
3. Which default GPO allows you to apply an Account Lockout Policy? Why?
4. If you want to configure auditing on domain controllers, which policy must you override or adjust? Why?
5. Which items can you redirect under Folder Redirection in Group Policy?
6. If you configure the Reset Account Lockout Counter After setting to zero, what does it mean?
7. On the Default Domain Controllers Policy, which audit policies are configured for No Auditing by default? What is the Policy Setting for the rest of the audit policies in the Default Domain Controllers Policy?

LAB CHALLENGE 8-1: MANAGING THE PASSWORD POLICY

Estimated completion time: 15 minutes

Company management has decided on a new company-wide security policy that they want you to implement.

Create a GPO that enforces company Password Policy as presented in the table below:

Policy	Policy Setting
Enforce Password History	2 passwords remembered
Maximum Password Age	30 days
Minimum Password Age	0 days
Minimum Password Length	7 characters
Password Must Meet Complexity Requirements	Enabled
Store Passwords Using Reversible Encryption	Disabled

NOTE You do not need to verify the reversible encryption or password age requirements.

LAB CHALLENGE 8-2: CONFIGURING THE ACCOUNT LOCKOUT POLICY

Estimated completion time: 15 minutes

You want to increase the security on your network by creating a more stringent Account Lockout Policy.

Configure a new GPO with an Account Lockout Policy that specifies the following:

Policy	Policy Setting
Account Lockout Duration	2 minutes
Account Lockout Threshold	1 invalid login attempt
Reset Account Lockout Counter After	2 minutes

NOTE *These settings can be found under Computer Configuration, Windows Settings, Security Settings, Account Policies, Account Lockout Policy in the GPO Editor.*

POST-LAB CLEANUP

Estimated completion time: 10 minutes

1. On the even# computer, open the Local Computer Policy by running gpedit.msc.
2. Set the Audit Object Access setting to No Auditing by clearing the Success and Failure check boxes (Reference 8-2).

   NOTE *This setting can be located in Computer Configuration, Windows Settings, Security Settings, Local Policies, Audit Policy.*

3. On the odd# computer, edit the DiskQuota1 GPO linked to the domain*xx*.local domain.
4. Open the Disk Quota settings modified in Exercise 8-4 to Disabled.

   NOTE *These settings can be located in Computer Configuration, Administrative Templates, System, Disk Quotas.*

5. In the right window pane, double-click Enable Disk Quotas. The Enable Disk Quotas Properties dialog box appears.
6. Select the Disabled radio button.
7. Click Next Setting. The Enforce Disk Quota Limit Properties dialog box appears.
8. Select the Disabled radio button.
9. Click Next Setting. The Default Quota Limit And Warning Level Properties dialog box appears.
10. Select the Disabled radio button and click OK.

11. Close the Group Policy Object Editor and the domain*xx*.local Properties dialog box.

12. Restart the odd# computer and then restart the even# computer while waiting for the odd# computer to complete its restart process.

13. On the odd# computer, log on as the default administrator of the domain*xx* domain.

14. Permanently remove all GPOs you created in this lab. In the domain*xx*.local domain, this includes PwdPol1, DiskQuota1, and any GPOs created in the Lab Challenges. In the Marketing OU, this includes Redirect1.

15. Delete the Marketing OU and the Lab8User objects it contains.

TROUBLESHOOTING LAB B

Troubleshooting Lab B is a practical application of the knowledge you have acquired from Chapters 5 through 8. Troubleshooting Lab B is divided into two sections, "Reviewing a Network" and "Troubleshooting a Break Scenario." In the "Reviewing a Network" section, you will review and assess a Windows Server 2003 Active Directory infrastructure for Contoso Pharmaceuticals. In the "Troubleshooting a Break Scenario" section, you will troubleshoot a particular break scenario. Your instructor or lab assistant has changed your computer configuration causing it to "break." Your task in this section will be to apply your acquired skills to troubleshoot and resolve the break.

REVIEWING A NETWORK

In this portion of Troubleshooting Lab B, you are a network administrator for Contoso Pharmaceuticals. The company network uses a single Active Directory domain named contoso.com. The company has operations in the United States, Canada, and Mexico. A single Active Directory site represents each of these operations. The sites are named: US_site, Can_site, and Mex_site.

The company has seven domain controllers running Windows Server 2003, Enterprise Edition, 15 member servers running Windows Server 2003, Standard Edition, and 500 client computers running Windows XP Professional. The domain functional level is Windows Server 2003. The Contoso Pharmaceuticals domain and organizational unit (OU) structure is as shown in Figure B-1.

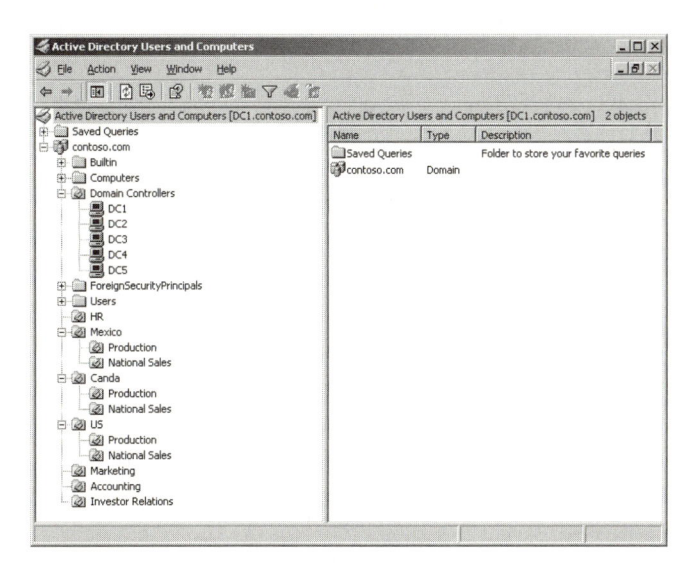

Figure B-1 Contoso Pharmaceuticals domain and OU structure

TROUBLESHOOTING LAB B

You are assigned to create the administrative structure for a new location in Singapore. You must implement smart cards for security logon. Eventually, Contoso Pharmaceuticals plans to implement smart cards throughout the company. All of the employees in Singapore have Singapore Personal Access (SingPass) identification accounts. You are expected to integrate their SingPass ID with their user identification. You cannot find an existing user property field that is appropriate for holding the SingPass. Furthermore, you are not allowed to deviate from Contoso Pharmaceutical's User Account Name and Location Policy, which specifies the following:

- Each user account should consist of a unique and sequential four-digit number, followed by a hyphen, a location designator, another hyphen, and two initials from the employee's name.

  For example, the first user account in the United States is 0001-US-DD, which was created for David Daniels. The second user account in the United States is 0002-US-CS, which was created for Candy Spoon.

- Each user account should be placed in an OU that represents his physical location.

  For example, the user accounts for network users located in Mexico should be placed in the Mexico OU.

- Administrator accounts for each location should be unique and sequential three-digit numbers, followed by a hyphen and a location designator.

  For example, the first three administrator accounts in Canada are named 001-Can, 002-Can, and 003-Can.

- All administrator accounts should be maintained in the default Users container.

The location designators are as shown in Table B-1.

Table B-1 **Location Designators for Contoso Pharmaceuticals**

Location	Designator
United States	US
Canada	Can
Mexico	Mex
Singapore	Sing

Based on what you know about Contoso Pharmaceuticals, answer each of the following questions:

1. Tai Yee is the first network user account that must be created in the Singapore OU. What user name do you expect to create for Tai Yee? Where would you place Tai Yee's user account in the Active Directory structure?

2. Mike Danseglio, a network administrator from Seattle, Washington, is the first network administrator in Singapore. He is living and working in Singapore for the first year of the operation. He needs an administrator account for the Singapore location. You want to delegate Mike full control

of the Singapore OU. However, you want Mike to have no control over his own account. What do you name his administrator account and where do you create it?

3. What Active Directory administrative units do you expect to create for the Singapore location, based on what already exists for the other locations?

4. What Active Directory wizard do you use to help distribute the administrative workload for the Singapore location? Where do you run this wizard?

5. How do you propose to maintain the SingPass identification for the Singapore employees in the Active Directory database?

6. A security consulting company performs an audit at the United States location while you are in Singapore. Your manager calls to say that the board has decided that all local administrator accounts should be renamed so that the account starts with 500 followed by a hyphen and the name of the location. How can you implement this change easily throughout the company?

7. All of the computers in the Singapore location have smart card readers built in with drivers that are compatible with Windows Server 2003 and Windows XP. If you want to distribute smart card certificates using autoenrollment to all users, what else must you configure?

8. You discover that another administrator has decided to distribute virus-scanning software to the entire company by linking a GPO to the domain. The virus-scanning software is not compatible with the computers in Singapore. You have different virus-scanning software that you want to deploy. What can you do to allow this software to be deployed to all other computers in the domain, except for the Singapore location?

9. The Singapore location has 10 computers that are dedicated for public and visitor use. However, employees with valid network logons might also use these computers. Although these systems are physically secure, you want to ensure that when employees use one of these public systems, they receive the same user settings as any public user. Public users are using a special guest account assigned by the receptionist at the Singapore location. What should you do to ensure that the limitations that apply to the special guest user account also apply to any user logging on to the public computers?

10. You want to ensure that users of the public computers are not allowed to fill up the hard disks with materials downloaded from the Internet. However, you want to allow guest users to save some information to these computers. What Group Policy solution can you use to control public users?

TROUBLESHOOTING A BREAK SCENARIO

In this portion of Troubleshooting Lab B, you must resolve a "break" that was introduced by your instructor or lab assistant. The computers you are assigned to fix are in pairs.

CAUTION *Do not proceed with this lab until you receive guidance from your instructor.* Your instructor or lab assistant will inform you which break scenario you will be performing (Break Scenario 1 or Break Scenario 2) and which computers to use. Your instructor or lab assistant may also have special instructions. Consult with your instructor before proceeding.

Break Scenario 1

You are a computer consultant who specializes in Active Directory. You are consulting for Contoso, Ltd. The company has locations in many different countries.

The company network contains five member servers running Windows Server 2003, Standard Edition, 200 client computers running Windows XP Professional, and three domain controllers running Windows Server 2003, Enterprise Edition. All computers are configured in a single Active Directory site.

You must resolve a configuration problem that affects every computer in the company. Users on the network cannot save more than 10 MB of data in their My Documents folders. The company finds this to be an extreme limitation and wants everyone to be able to save as much data as necessary to the My Documents folder, or anywhere else on the computer, with no tracking or limitation.

TIP Your solution to this problem is to leave no GPO links in place after the problem is solved. Furthermore, do not modify the Default Domain Controllers Policy or the Default Domain Policy when troubleshooting this problem.

As you resolve this configuration issue, fill out the worksheet in the TroubleshootingLabB folder and include the following information:

- Description of the issue
- A list of all steps taken to try and diagnose the problem, even the ones that did not work
- Description of the problem
- Description of the solution
- List of the tools and resources you used to help solve this problem

Break Scenario 2

You are a computer consultant specializing in Active Directory. You are consulting for Contoso, Ltd. The company has locations in many different countries.

The company network contains five member servers running Windows Server 2003, Standard Edition, 200 client computers running Windows XP Professional, and three domain controllers running Windows Server 2003, Enterprise Edition. All computers are configured in a single Active Directory site.

You are assigned to resolve a configuration issue that affects a user named Julie, as well as 500 other employees in the company. Julie's My Documents folder is redirected to a central location. However, company policy states that all users' My Documents folders should be maintained on their local computers.

TIP Julie's user name is Julie, and her password is MSPress#1. Your solution should not only resolve Julie's problem, it should resolve the problem for all computers and users in the domain.

As you resolve this configuration issue, fill out the worksheet in the TroubleshootingLabB folder and include the following information:

- Description of the issue
- A list of all steps taken to try and diagnose the problem, even the ones that did not work
- Description of the problem
- Description of the solution
- List of the tools and resources you used to help solve this problem

LAB 9
SOFTWARE DISTRIBUTION

This lab contains the following exercises and activities:

- Exercise 9-1: Deploying Software to Users
- Exercise 9-2: Using Software Restriction Policies
- Exercise 9-3: Deploying Software to Computers
- Lab Review Questions
- Lab Challenge 9-1: Deploying Administrative Tools
- Lab Challenge 9-2: Restricting Access to Cmd

SCENARIO

You are a network administrator for Blue Yonder Airlines. Blue Yonder Airlines has a single Active Directory domain named blueyonderairlines.com. There are three domain controllers on the network. The domain controllers run Windows Server 2003, Standard Edition. There are 10 member servers on the domain. Two of the member servers run Windows Server 2003, Enterprise Edition, and the rest run Windows Server 2003, Standard Edition. The 400 client computers on the domain run Microsoft Windows XP Professional.

Corporate management decides that all of the applications throughout the company must be standardized. Furthermore, management publishes a list of prohibited applications. Your task is to ensure that the standardized applications are deployed appropriately and that the prohibited applications are not used.

After completing this lab, you will be able to:

- Deploy software packages to domain users and computers
- Assign software packages to users and computers
- Publish software packages to users
- Configure Software Restriction Policies
- Implement path rules
- Implement hash rules

Estimated lesson time: 130 minutes

> **NOTE** In this lab, you will see the characters xx, yy, and zz. These directions assume that you are working on computers configured in pairs and that each computer has a number. One number is odd and the other number is even. For example, Computer01 is the odd# computer and Computer02 is the even# computer. When you see xx, substitute the unique number assigned to the odd# computer. When you see yy, substitute the unique number assigned to the even# computer. When you see zz, substitute the number assigned to the computer at which you are working, either odd or even.
>
> Whenever you see the Manage Your Server page appear in this lab, select the Don't Display This Page At Logon check box and close the Manage Your Server page.

LAB DEPENDENCIES

In order to complete this lab, you must be sure that the following is done:

- The even# computer must be configured to use the odd# computer as its Preferred DNS Server, as explained in Lab Exercise 1-4.
- Active Directory is installed on the odd# computer. Lab Exercise 2-1 covers the installation of Active Directory on the odd# computer.
- The even# computer must be a member of the odd# computer's domain, as shown in Lab Exercise 2-3.
- The even# computer must not be a domain controller for the child domain. If the even# computer is a domain controller for the child domain, you must demote it as shown in Lab Exercise 7-1.

EXERCISE 9-1: DEPLOYING SOFTWARE TO USERS

Estimated completion time: 35 minutes

Corporate management decides that users in the domain should be able to install a custom application that has an associated .msi package. In this lab, you use the admigration.msi tool to represent the software package that your managers want you to distribute.

Preparing the Distribution Share:

1. On the odd# computer, log on as the default administrator of the domain*xx* domain.

2. On the odd# computer, insert the Windows Server 2003 installation CD-ROM in to the CD-ROM drive. If the Welcome screen appears, click Exit.

3. Open the following location: C:\Lab Manual\Lab09. Double-click the Ex9-1.bat file. This file creates a folder on the C: drive named MSI and shares that folder to the Everyone group. This file also copies the ADMIGRATION.MSI and GPMC.MSI files into the C:\MSI folder.

Publishing Software

1. On the odd# computer, open Active Directory Users And Computers.
2. In the left window pane, right-click the domain*xx*.local object. Click Properties. The domain*xx*.local Properties dialog box appears.
3. Click the Group Policy tab.
4. Click New. A New Group Policy Object appears under the Group Policy Object Links column.
5. Type **SOFTDIST1** and press ENTER.
6. Click Edit.
7. In the left window pane, under the User Configuration object, expand the Software Settings object.
8. Right-click Software Installation object and click Properties. The Software Installation Properties dialog box appears.
9. Click the Categories tab. Click Add. The Enter New Category dialog box appears.
10. Type **Active Directory Tools** and click OK as shown in the following figure.

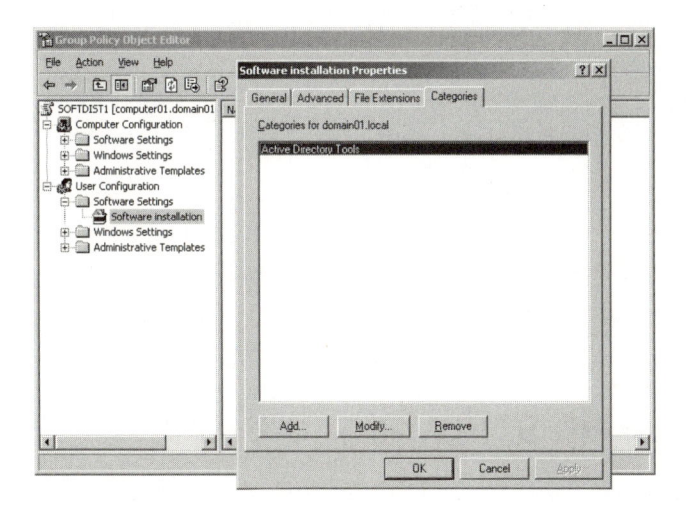

11. In the Software Installation Properties dialog box, click OK.
12. Right-click Software Installation, click New and then Package. The Open dialog box appears.
13. Click the File Name text box.
14. Type **\\computer*xx*\msi** and press ENTER.
15. Click ADMIGRATION.MSI and then click Open. The Deploy Software dialog box appears as shown in the following figure.

124   LAB 9:   SOFTWARE DISTRIBUTION

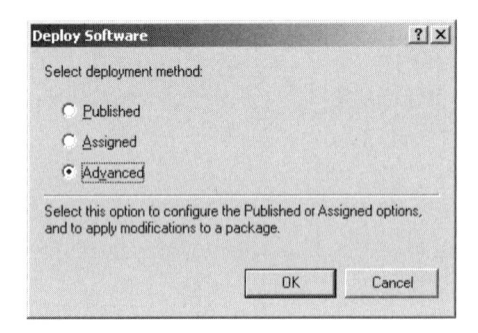

16. Select the Advanced radio button and click OK. After a few moments, the Active Directory Migration Tool Properties dialog box appears.

17. Click the Deployment tab. Verify that the Published radio button is selected under Deployment Type as shown in the following figure.

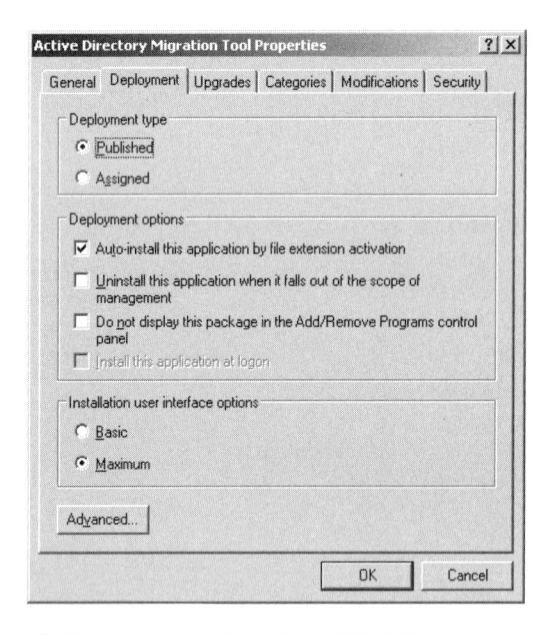

18. Click the Categories tab. Click Select to move the Active Directory Tools category over to the Selected Categories column. Click OK.

19. Close the Group Policy Object Editor.

20. Close the domain*xx*.local Properties dialog box.

Checking for Published Software

1. On the even# computer, log on as the default administrator of the domain*xx* domain.

2. Click Start, click Control Panel, and then click Add Or Remove Programs. The Add Or Remove Programs tool appears.

3. Click the Add New Programs icon on the left side of the Add Or Remove Programs tool.

4. Select Active Directory Tools in the Category selection box.

    QUESTION   Do you see the Active Directory Migration Tool listed?

    QUESTION   Is the Active Directory Migration tool installed?

5. Close the Add Or Remove Programs tool.

6. Click Start, point to All Programs, and then click Administrative Tools.

   QUESTION Do you see the Active Directory Migration Tool listed?

7. Log off.

Assigning Software

1. On the odd# computer, open the domain*xx*.local Properties dialog box from within Active Directory Users And Computers.

2. Click the Group Policy tab.

3. Click the SOFTDIST1 GPO link and then click Edit.

4. In the left window pane, under the User Configuration object, expand the Software Settings object.

5. In the left window pane, click the Software Installation object.

6. In the right window pane, right-click Active Directory Migration Tool and click Assign.

7. Close the Group Policy Object Editor.

8. In the domain*xx*.local Properties dialog box click OK.

Checking for Assigned Software

1. On the even# computer, log on as the default administrator of the domain*xx* domain.

2. Click Start, point to All Programs, and then click Administrative Tools.

   QUESTION Do you see the Active Directory Migration Tool listed?

   NOTE Be careful not to click on the Active Directory Migration Tool. This will change the results of the following steps.

3. Right-click the Active Directory Migration Tool and then click Properties.

4. Read the information presented to you.

   QUESTION Is the Active Directory Migration Tool currently installed on this computer? What indicator do you see here?

5. Click Cancel.

6. Click Start, point to All Programs, Administrative Tools, and then click Active Directory Migration Tool. The Active Directory Migration Tool Setup wizard appears.

7. Use the Active Directory Migration Tool Setup Wizard to complete the installation.

8. After the installation, the Active Directory Migration Tool opens automatically, close the tool.

9. Click Start, point to All Programs, and then click Administrative Tools.

10. Right-click the Active Directory Migration Tool and then click Properties.

11. Read the information presented to you.

   QUESTION Is the Active Directory Migration Tool currently installed on this computer? How do you know?

12. Click Cancel and log off the even# computer.

EXERCISE 9-2: USING SOFTWARE RESTRICTION POLICIES

Estimated completion time: 25 minutes

Corporate management has decided that too many users are spending time drawing pictures in Microsoft Paint when they should be working. You need to prevent users from accessing Microsoft Paint. You decide to try and accomplish this by using Software Restriction Policies.

Path Rule

1. On the odd# computer, open the domain*xx*.local Properties dialog box from within Active Directory Users And Computers.

2. Click the Group Policy tab.

3. Click New. A New Group Policy Object appears under Group Policy Object Links column.

4. Type **SRP1** and press ENTER.

5. Click Edit.

6. In the left window pane, under the User Configuration object, expand the Windows Settings, Security Settings, and Software Restriction Policies objects.

7. Right-click Software Restriction Policies object and click New Software Restriction Policies.

8. In the left window pane, select the Additional Rules object. The default rules are displayed in the right window pane. Right-click the Additional Rules object and then click New Path Rule.

9. In the Path box, type **C:\WINDOWS\system32\mspaint.exe.** Ensure that the Security Level remains set to Disallowed.

10. Click OK. The new path rule appears in the right window pane.

11. Close the Group Policy Object Editor and close the domain*xx*.local Properties dialog box.

12. On the even# computer, log on as the default administrator of the domain*xx* domain.

13. Click Start, point to All Programs, then Accessories, and click Paint. A message box appears.

14. Read the message and click OK.

QUESTION Why did the computer fail to open mspaint.exe?

QUESTION Can you find a way around this rule that would enable users to run mspaint.exe?

Testing the Path Rule

1. On the even# computer, open a command prompt window.

2. Type **copy C:\WINDOWS\system32\mspaint.exe c:** in the command prompt window and press ENTER.

3. Type **C:\mspaint.exe** in the command prompt window and press ENTER.

   QUESTION What happens?

Hash Rule

1. On the odd# computer, open the domain*xx*.local Properties dialog box from within Active Directory Users And Computers.

2. Click the Group Policy tab.

3. Click New. A New Group Policy Object appears under Group Policy Object Links column.

4. Type **SRP2** and press ENTER.

5. Click Edit.

6. In the left window pane, under the User Configuration object, expand the Windows Settings, Security Settings, and Software Restriction Policies objects.

7. Right-click the Software Restriction Policies object and click New Software Restriction Policies.

8. In the left window pane, select the Additional Rules object. The default rules are displayed in the right window pane. Right-click the Additional Rules object and then click New Hash Rule. The New Hash Rule dialog box appears.

9. Click Browse. The Open dialog box appears.

10. In the File Name text box, type **C:\WINDOWS\system32\mspaint.exe**. Click Open.

11. In the New Hash Rule dialog box click OK as shown in the following figure.

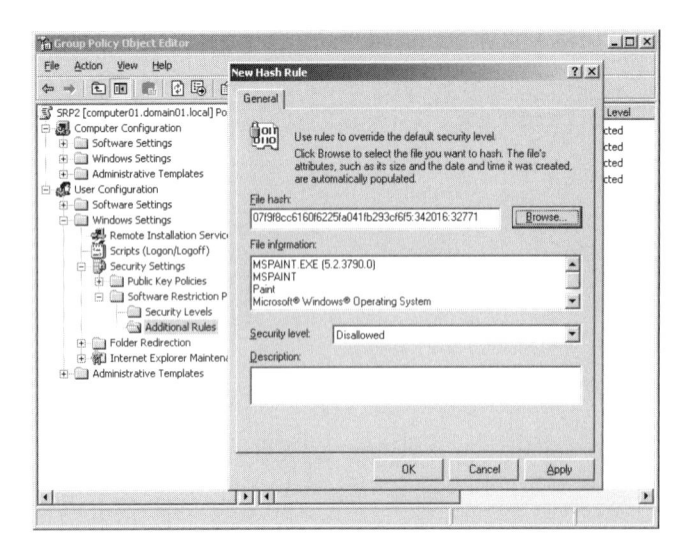

12. Close the Group Policy Object Editor and the domain*xx*.local Properties dialog box.

13. On the even# computer, log off and log on as the default administrator of the domain*xx* domain to update Group Policy User Settings.

14. Open a command prompt window.

15. Type **c:\mspaint.exe** and press ENTER.

    QUESTION *Can you run the copy of mspaint.exe now? Why?*

EXERCISE 9-3: DEPLOYING SOFTWARE TO COMPUTERS

Estimated completion time: 20 minutes

You want to deploy the Group Policy Management Console (GPMC) to all computers on your domain.

1. On the odd# computer, ensure that you are still logged on as the default administrator of the domain*xx* domain.

2. If necessary, open Active Directory Users and Computers. Right-click the domain*xx*.local object and click Properties.

3. Click the Group Policy tab.

4. Click New. A New Group Policy Object appears under the Group Policy Object Links column.

5. Type **DeployGPMC** and press ENTER.

6. Click Edit.

7. In the left window pane, under the Computer Configuration object, expand the Software Settings object.

8. Right-click Software Installation, click New, and then click Package. The Open dialog box appears.

9. Click the File Name text box.

10. Type **\\computer*xx*\msi** and press ENTER.
11. Click gpmc.msi and then click Open. The Deploy Software dialog box appears as shown in the following figure.
12. Verify that the Assigned radio button is selected and click OK.
13. Close the Group Policy Object Editor and the domain*xx*.local Properties dialog box.
14. Restart the even# computer.
15. On the even# computer, log on as the default administrator of the domain*xx* domain.
16. Click Start and then click Run. Type **gpmc.msc** and press ENTER. The Group Policy Management Console opens.
17. In the left window pane, expand the Forest object.
18. Right-click Group Policy Results and click Group Policy Results Wizard. The Group Policy Results Wizard appears.
19. Click Next. The Computer Selection page appears.
20. Click Next. The User Selection page appears.
21. Click Next. The Summary Of Selections page appears.
22. Click Next and then click Finish. A report is generated. After a few moments, an Internet Explorer message box appears.
23. Read the message and click Add. A Trusted Sites dialog box appears.
24. Click Add and then Close.
25. In the right window pane, click the Settings tab.
26. Under Computer Configuration, click Show where you see Installed Applications.

    QUESTION Do you see the Group Policy Management Console among the list of Installed Applications?

27. Close the Group Policy Management console.

    NOTE If you plan to do the Lab Challenges, do not restart the odd# computer. If you restart the odd# computer, the Group Policy Management Console will be installed automatically on restart. If the Group Policy Management Console is installed, you won't be able to follow all the steps in the Lab Challenges.

LAB REVIEW QUESTIONS

Estimated completion time: 15 minutes

1. In your words, describe what you learned during this lab.
2. Is the option to publish a software package to a computer available when you create a software package?
3. How can you enable the option Install This Application At Logon in a software package's Deployment tab?
4. What are the advantages and disadvantages of using path rules?
5. What can a hash rule do that a path rule cannot? What is a limitation of a hash rule?

LAB CHALLENGE 9-1: DEPLOYING ADMINISTRATIVE TOOLS

Estimated completion time: 15 minutes

You decide that everyone should have access to the administrative tools on your domain. You want to deploy the administrative tools to all users using a GPO that is linked to the domain, but is not the Default Domain Policy.

- Your GPO name should be SOFTDIST2 and you should configure it to deploy the Administrative Tools (adminpak.msi) to every computer on the domain.

LAB CHALLENGE 9-2: RESTRICTING ACCESS TO CMD

Estimated completion time: 15 minutes

Although you lock down the desktop using Group Policy, you see copies of Cmd.exe on users' desktops. You are not sure how these files are getting there, but you want to ensure that users cannot run Cmd.exe, so you want to create a hash rule to stop users from running this program on the domain.

- Create a GPO named SRP3 and link it to the domain. Edit the GPO and create a hash rule for all computers that disallows the use of Cmd.exe.

POST-LAB CLEANUP

Estimated completion time: 5 minutes

Remove all software distribution packages you deployed in this lab except the deployment of DeployGPMC that was done in Lab Exercise 9-3.

1. Restart the odd# computer.
2. On the odd# computer, log on as the default administrator of the domain*xx* domain.
3. Open Active Directory Users And Computers.

4. Right-click the domain*xx*.local object and click Properties.
5. Click the Group Policy tab.

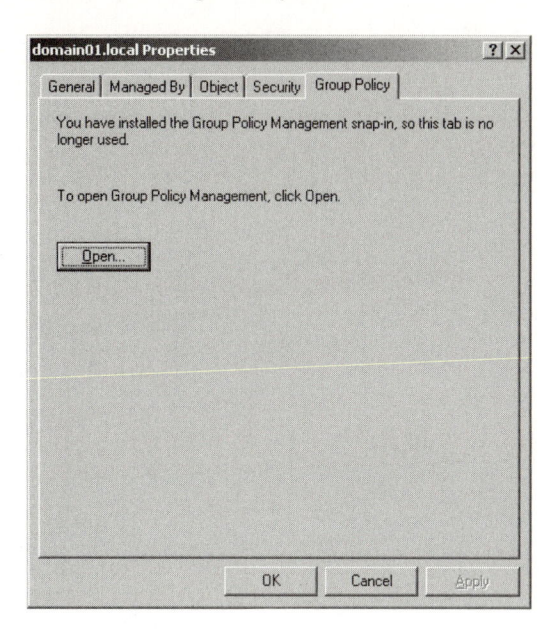

NOTE If the Group Policy tab does not have an Open button, the Group Policy Management Console is not installed.

6. Click Open. The Group Policy Management Console opens.
7. Expand Forest, Domains, domain*xx*.local, and Group Policy Objects. Several GPOs appear.

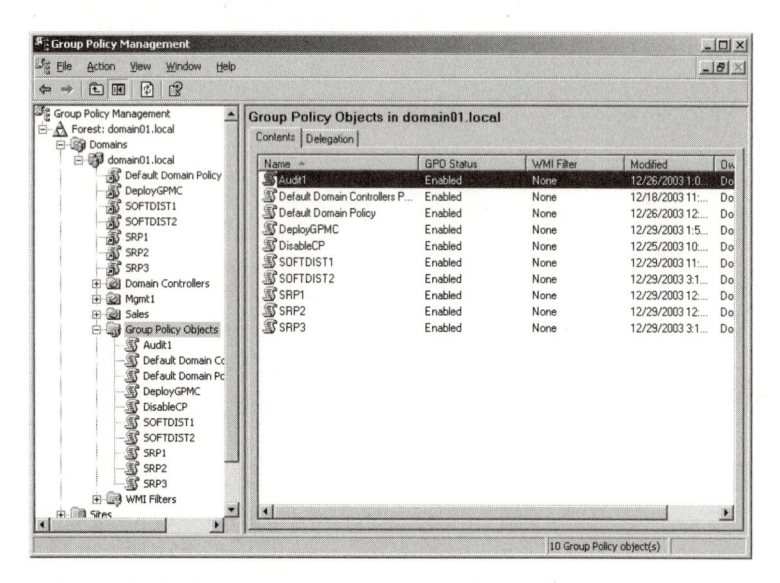

8. Delete all of the GPOs you see listed here, except the Default Domain Controllers Policy, Default Domain Policy, and the DeployGMPC GPOs. To delete a GPO, select the object that represents the GPO by clicking that object and then press the Delete key on your keyboard. Click OK when you see the Group Policy Management message box asking you to confirm deletion.
9. Once you are finished, close all open windows and restart both computers.

LAB 10
CONTROLLING GROUP POLICY

This lab contains the following exercises and activities:

- Exercise 10-1: Gpresult and RSoP
- Exercise 10-2: Using Security Filtering
- Exercise 10-3: Working with WMI filters
- Lab Review Questions
- Lab Challenge 10-1: Applying Security Filtering
- Lab Challenge 10-2: Applying WMI Filtering

SCENARIO

You are a network administrator for Consolidated Messenger. The company network has a single Active Directory domain named consolidatedmessenger.com. There are five domain controllers, 10 member servers, and 500 client computers in consolidatedmessenger.com. All of the client computers run Microsoft Windows XP Professional. All of the member servers and domain controllers run Windows Server 2003, Standard Edition.

You are responsible for managing Group Policy for Consolidated Messenger. You use Group Policy to deploy and maintain applications, control user access to software, and standardize desktops throughout the company. However, you find there are many times when you want a policy to apply or not apply to a certain user, computer, or group of users and computers. Management does not want you to change the current organizational unit (OU) structure, and you do not want to enable Block Policy Inheritance more than necessary. Therefore, you are interested in using security filtering and WMI filters as a means of controlling Group Policy deployments.

After completing this lab, you will be able to:

- Use the Group Policy Management Console (GPMC) to configure, link, edit, and delete Group Policy Objects (GPOs)
- Use Gpresult and RSoP to determine how GPOs are deployed and filtered.
- Implement Group Policy security filtering
- Configure WMI filters and link them to Group Policy Objects

Estimated lesson time: 120 minutes

LAB DEPENDENCIES

In order to complete this lab, you must be sure that the following are done:

- The even# computer must be configured to use the odd# computer as its Preferred DNS Server, as explained in Lab Exercise 1-4.
- Active Directory is installed on the odd# computer. Lab Exercise 2-1 covers the installation of Active Directory on the odd# computer.
- The even# computer must be a member of the odd# computer's domain, as shown in Lab Exercise 2-3.
- Support Tools must be installed, as described in Lab Exercise 3-1
- Members of the Domain Users group have the right to log on to domain controllers. Lab Exercise 4-1 explains how to complete this configuration.
- The domain functional level must be Windows 2000 native, which is described in Lab Exercise 4-2.
- The even# computer must not be a domain controller for the child domain. If the even# computer is a domain controller for the child domain, you must demote it, as shown in Lab Exercise 7-1.
- The Group Policy Management Console (GPMC) should be deployed to all computers in your domain, as shown in Lab Exercise 9-3.

NOTE *In this lab you will see the characters xx, yy, and zz. These directions assume that you are working on computers configured in pairs and that each computer has a number. One number is odd and the other number is even. For example, Computer01 is the odd# computer and Computer02 is the even# computer. When you see xx, substitute the unique number assigned to the odd# computer. When you see yy, substitute the unique number assigned to the even# computer. When you see zz, substitute the number assigned to the computer at which you are working, either odd or even.*

Whenever you see the Manage Your Server page appear in this lab, select the Don't Display This Page At Logon check box and close the Manage Your Server page.

EXERCISE 10-1: GPRESULT AND RSOP

Estimated completion time: 25 minutes

In addition to managing Group Policy, you must often trace the application of GPOs to specific computers or users. Use the Gpresult and Rsop.msc tools to assist in troubleshooting GPO deployment issues.

In this lab you use the organizational units (OUs), user accounts, and Group Policy Objects (GPOs) listed in Table 10-1. Your first task is to create this structure.

Table 10-1 OU Structure

OU	Users	GPO	GPO Settings	GPO Links
10A	10Auser1 10Auser2	GPOA	Remove Run Enabled	10A
10B	10Buser1 10Buser2	GPOB	Remove Help Enabled	10B
10C	10Cuser1 10Cuser2	GPOC	Remove Search Enabled	10C

Creating the OU Structure

1. On the odd# computer, log on as the default administrator of the domain*xx* domain.

2. Using Active Directory Users And Computers, create three organizational units (OUs), as listed in Table 10-1 (reference Exercise 6-3). OU 10A and OU 10B should be top-level OUs subordinate to the domain. OU 10C should be subordinate to OU 10B.

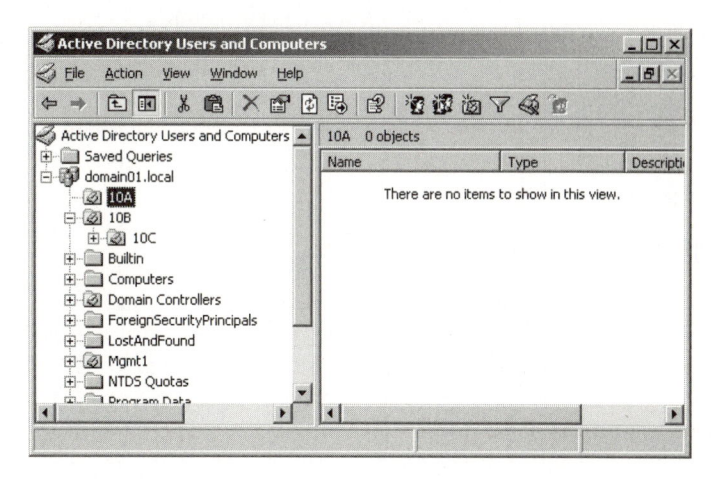

3. Create six user accounts in the appropriate OUs as listed in Table 10-1 (reference Lab Exercise 4-1). Set all user passwords to **MSPress#1**. Do not require users to change their passwords at the next logon.

4. Right-click the 10A OU and click Properties. The 10A Properties dialog box appears.

5. Click the Group Policy tab. Notice that the options have changed now that the Group Policy Management Console (GPMC) is installed.

NOTE *If the Group Policy Management Console (GPMC) is not installed you must install it at this point in order to follow these instructions. You can install the GPMC either by double-clicking the gpmc.msi file in the Lab09 folder, or by completing Exercise 9-3.*

6. Click Open. The Group Policy Management Console appears.

7. Right-click the 10A OU and click Create And Link A GPO Here. The New GPO dialog box appears.

8. Type **GPOA** in the Name text box and click OK. In the right window pane, GPOA appears.

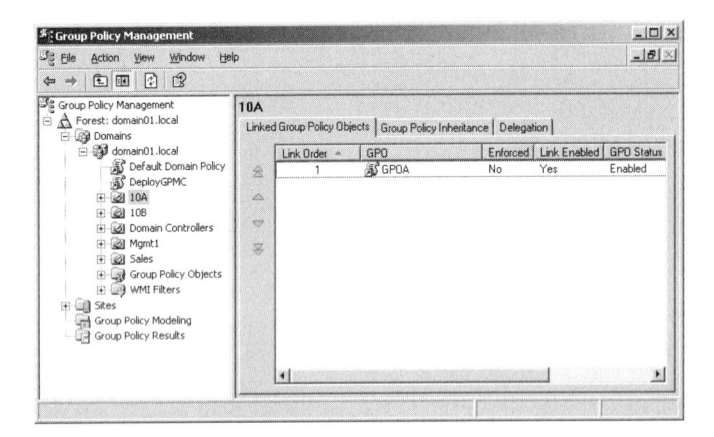

9. Right-click GPOA and click Edit. The Group Policy Object Editor appears.

10. In the left window pane, under User Configuration expand Administrative Templates, and then click on the Start Menu And Taskbar object.

11. In the right window pane, double-click Remove Run Menu From Start Menu. The Remove Run Menu From Start Menu Properties dialog box appears.

12. Select the Enabled radio button and click OK.

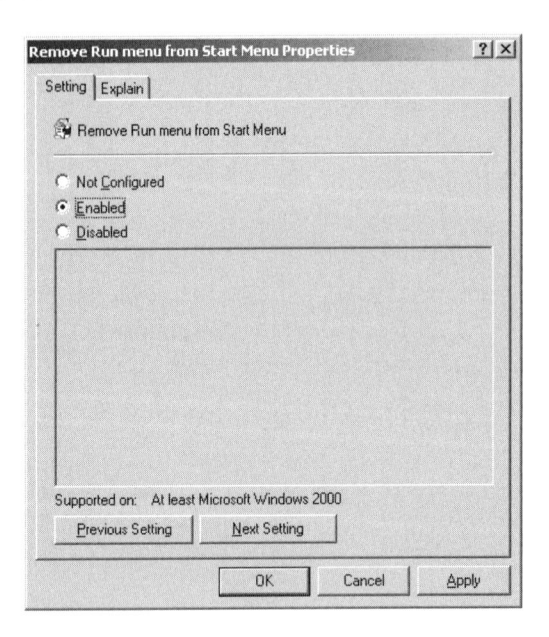

13. Close the Group Policy Object Editor, but do not close the Group Policy Management Console.

14. Use the Group Policy Management Console to create and link another GPO, but this time to the 10B OU. This new GPO should be named GPOB. Edit GPOB and enable the Remove Help Menu From Start Menu setting.

15. Use the Group Policy Management Console to create and link one more GPO, but this time to the 10C OU. This new GPO should be named GPOC. Edit GPOC and enable the Remove Search Menu From Start Menu setting.

Using Gpresult to Troubleshoot Deployment

1. On the odd# computer, log off and log on as 10Auser1 of the domain*xx* domain.

    NOTE *The Run menu is missing from the Start menu. You must click Start, All Programs, Accessories, and Command Prompt to open a command prompt window.*

2. Open a command prompt window, type **gpresult,** and then press ENTER. After a couple minutes, output will appear in the command prompt window.

3. Look at the Applied Group Policy Objects section and verify that GPOA is listed.

4. Close the command prompt window.

5. On the even# computer, log on as 10Auser2 of the domain*xx* domain. Repeat steps 2 – 4.

Using RSoP to Troubleshoot Deployment

1. On the odd# computer, log off and log on as 10Cuser1 of the domain*xx* domain.

2. Click Start and then click Run.

3. Run RSoP, by typing **rsop.msc** in the Run dialog box and then clicking OK. A Group Policy error message is displayed. This occurs because this user does not have the administrative permissions to see what security settings are applied to the computer. However, this user is allowed to see the settings applying to the user account.

4. Read the error message and then click Close. The Resultant Set Of Policy console appears.

5. In the left window pane, expand Administrative Templates, and click Start Menu And Taskbar.

6. Read the content in the right window pane. You should see only the GPO settings that apply to this user account.

    QUESTION *What are the names of the settings that apply to this user account?*

7. In the right window pane, double-click Remove Help Menu From Start Menu. The Remove Help Menu From Start Menu Properties dialog box appears.

8. Click the Precedence tab.

   QUESTION What GPO name do you see listed here?

9. Click OK to close the Remove Help Menu From Start Menu Properties dialog box.

10. Close the Resultant Set Of Policy console.

11. On the even# computer, log off and log on as 10Cuser2 of the domain*xx* domain. Repeat steps 2 – 10.

12. On the odd# computer, log off and log on as the default administrator of the domain*xx* domain.

13. Run Rsop.msc.

    QUESTION Do you see the error message that the user accounts received? Explain any differences you discover.

14. Close the Resultant Set Of Policy console.

EXERCISE 10-2: USING SECURITY FILTERING

Estimated completion time: 20 minutes

You have a GPO that you want to apply to only members of 10Bgroup1 in the 10B OU. You want to try security filtering to see if you can prevent this GPO from applying to other users.

Using 10Bgroup1 for Security Filtering

1. On the odd# computer, open Active Directory Users And Computers.

2. Expand domain*xx*.local in the left window pane.

3. Right-click the 10B OU, click New, and then click Group. The New Object – Group dialog box appears.

4. In the Group Name text box, type **10Bgroup1** and click OK.

   NOTE To use the drag-and-drop method to add a user account to a group, you must have the View Users, Groups, And Computers As Containers option enabled. Click the View menu and ensure there is a check mark next to the Users, Groups, And Computers As Containers option. If not, click that option. If you view it again, you should see the check mark.

5. Ensure that the 10B OU is selected in the left window pane. Use the drag-and-drop method to add 10Buser1 to the 10Bgroup1 group. Click OK when you receive confirmation that the user is added.

6. Right-click the 10B OU in the left window pane and click Properties. The 10B Properties dialog box appears.

7. Click the Group Policy tab and then click Open. The Group Policy Management Console appears.

8. Expand the 10B OU in the left window pane.

9. In the left window pane, click GPOB. At this point, you may see a Group Policy Management Console message appear. If that happens, read the message, select the Do Not Show This Message Again check box, and click OK.

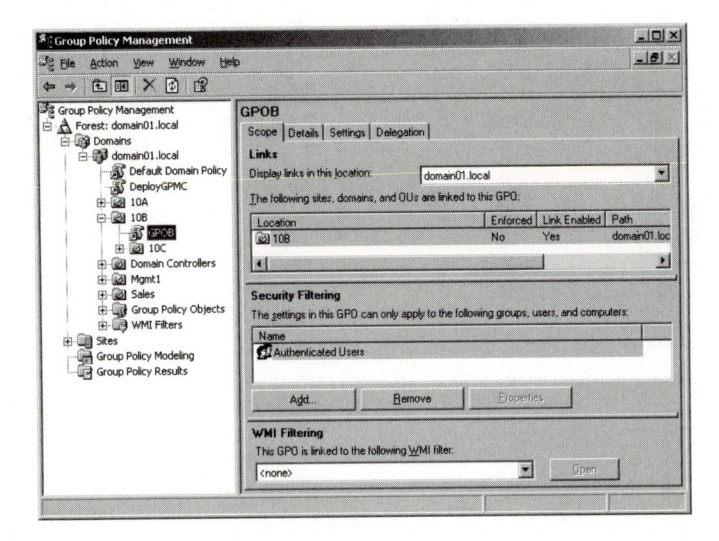

10. In the right window pane, you should see the Scope tab displayed. Click Authenticated Users under the heading Security Filtering and then click Remove. A Group Policy Management message appears asking you to confirm the removal. Click OK

11. Click Add under the Security Filtering heading. The Select User, Computer Or Group dialog box appears.

12. Type **10Bgroup1** in the Enter The Object Name To Select text box and click Check Names. Verify that 10Bgroup1 is underlined and click OK.

13. Click on the Delegation tab near the top of the right window pane. Click the Advanced button in the lower right corner of the window. The GPOB Security Settings dialog box opens.

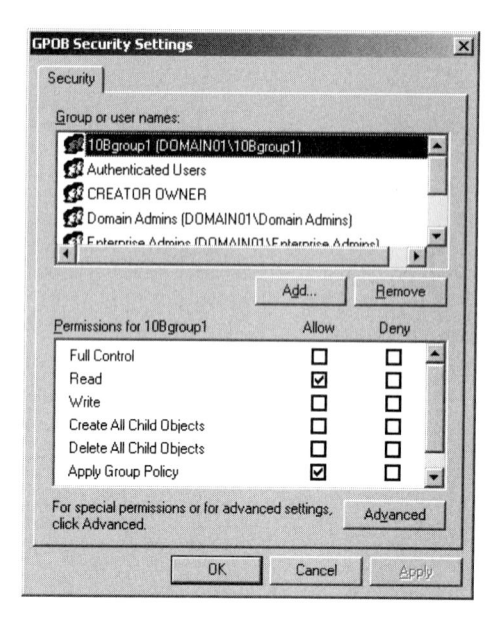

14. Review the Permissions that are allowed for 10Bgroup1. This group should have the Read and Apply Group Policy permissions set to Allow. Click OK.

15. Click the Scope tab again.

    QUESTION *Compare and contrast the Security Filtering section and the Security Settings dialog box. Specifically, how are the two items related and in what ways do they differ?*

16. Close the Group Policy Management Console.

17. In the 10B Properties dialog box, click OK.

18. Close Active Directory Users And Computers.

19. Log off both the odd# and even# computers.

Testing Security Filtering

1. On the odd# computer, log on as 10Buser1 of the domain*xx* domain.

2. Run Gpresult from a command prompt window and review the objects listed in the Applied Group Policy Objects section (reference Exercise 10-1).

3. Run Rsop.msc to validate which configuration settings affect 10Buser1 (reference Exercise 10-1).

4. Click Start.

    QUESTION *Do you have the Help And Support menu available?*

5. On the even# computer, log on as 10Buser2 of the domain*xx* domain.

6. Run Gpresult from a command prompt window and review the objects listed in the Applied Group Policy Objects section (reference Exercise 10-1).

7. Run Rsop.msc to validate which configuration settings affect 10Buser2 (reference Exercise 10-1).

    QUESTION *Why does 10Buser2 have a Help And Support menu in the Start menu, but 10Buser1 does not?*

    QUESTION *If you want the GPO to apply to all authenticated users in the 10B OU and subordinate OUs except the members of 10Bgroup1, what must you do differently?*

8. Log off both the odd# and even# computers.

EXERCISE 10-3: WORKING WITH WMI FILTERS

Estimated completion time: 25 minutes

There are several computers on your network that you want to remove the last logged on user name from the Log On To Windows dialog box. All of these computers already have the Task Scheduler service disabled. You decide to create a GPO with a WMI filter to remove the user name from the Log On To Windows dialog box if the Task Scheduler service is disabled.

Creating a GPO That Uses a WMI Filter

1. On the even# computer, log on as the default administrator of the domain*xx* domain.

2. Open a command prompt window, type **net stop schedule**, and then press ENTER. This stops the Task Scheduler service.

3. Type **sc config schedule start= disabled**, and then press ENTER. You should see a message that reads [SC] ChangeServiceConfig SUCCESS.

    NOTE *If you do not receive the confirmation message indicating success, ensure that you have a space between the start= and disabled portions of the command.*

4. On the odd# computer, log on as the default administrator of the domain*xx* domain.

5. Open the Active Directory Users And Computers console.

6. Right-click domain*xx*.local and click Properties. The domain*xx*.local Properties dialog box appears.

7. Click the Group Policy tab and then click Open. The Group Policy Management Console appears.

8. Right-click domain*xx*.local and then click Create And Link A GPO Here. The New GPO dialog box appears.

9. Type **GPOD** into the Name text box and click OK. In the right window pane, GPOD appears.

10. Right-click GPOD in the right window pane and click Edit. The Group Policy Object Editor appears.

11. In the left window pane, under the Computer Configuration object, expand Windows Settings, Security Settings, and Local Policies. Click Security Options.

12. In the right window pane, double-click Interactive Logon: Do Not Display Last User Name.

13. Select the Define This Policy Setting check box and then select the Enabled radio button.

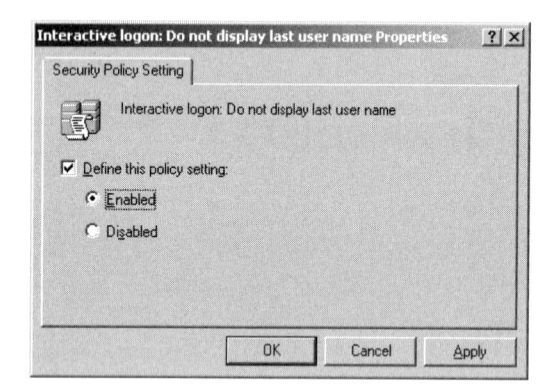

14. Click OK and then close the Group Policy Object Editor.

15. In the left window pane of the Group Policy Management Console, right-click WMI Filters and click New. The New WMI Filter dialog box appears.

16. Type **Task Scheduler Disabled** in the Name text box of the New WMI Filter dialog box.

17. Click Add. The WMI Query dialog box appears.

18. Type **Select * from Win32_Service where Name='schedule' and startmode='disabled'** in the Query text box and click OK.

19. Click Save in the New WMI Filter dialog box.

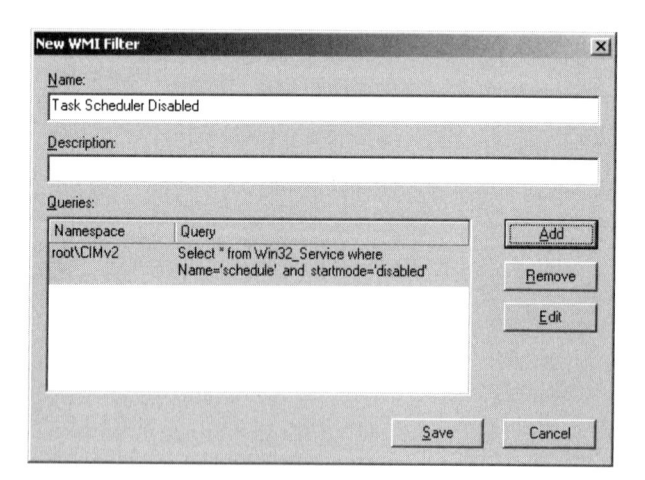

20. In the left window pane, click GPOD, which is displayed just below domainxx.local. If a Group Policy Management Console message appears, click OK.

21. In the right window pane, click the drop-down selection box below the WMI Filtering heading and select the Task Scheduler Disabled WMI filter. A Group Policy Management message appears, asking you to confirm this change. Click Yes.
22. Close the Group Policy Management Console.
23. Click OK to close the domain*xx*.local Properties dialog box.
24. Close Active Directory Users And Computers.

Testing the WMI Filter
1. On the even# computer, open a command prompt window.
2. Type **gpupdate** in the command prompt window and press ENTER.
3. Close the command prompt window and log off.
4. Press CTRL + ALT + DELETE to display the Log On To Windows dialog box.

   QUESTION   *Do you see the user name of the last person to log on to this computer? Explain your results.*

5. On the odd# computer, open a command prompt window, type **gpupdate**, and press ENTER.
6. Type **wmic service where startmode='auto' get name** and press ENTER. You will probably see a message that asks you to wait while WMIC is installed. After this, you should see a report of services configured to run automatically at startup. Notice the list of services that are configured to start includes Schedule, which is the Task Scheduler service.
7. Close the command prompt window and log off.
8. Press CTRL + ALT + DELETE to display the Log On To Windows dialog box.

   QUESTION   *Do you see the user name of the last person to log on to this computer? Explain your results.*

LAB REVIEW QUESTIONS

Estimated completion time: 15 minutes
1. In your words, describe what you learned during this lab.
2. When you want to filter a GPO based on file system or services running, what type of filtering do you use?
3. When you want to filter a GPO based on group membership, what type of filter do you use?
4. What tools can you use to investigate the application of GPOs for a particular computer or user account?
5. When running Gpresult, or GPMC, using a non-administrative account, what information is unavailable?

LAB CHALLENGE 10-1: APPLYING SECURITY FILTERING

Estimated completion time: 10 minutes

You want to prevent users who are not members of 10Cgroup1 from receiving GPOC.

Your task is to create a group named 10Cgroup1 in the 10C OU. Add the user account 10Cuser2 to 10Cgroup1. Create a security filter so that user accounts that are members of the 10Cgroup1 are the only user accounts affected by GPOC. Verify that 10Cuser1 has the Search menu in the Start menu. Use Rsop.msc to verify that the policy is correctly deployed.

LAB CHALLENGE 10-2: APPLYING WMI FILTERING

Estimated completion time: 25 minutes

Your task is to disable the Computer Browser (browser) service on the even# computer. Create a GPO named GPOE. In GPOE, configure the Security Option Interactive Logon Do Not Require CTRL + ALT + DEL To Logon to be enabled. Create a WMI filter so that computers that do not have the Computer Browser service enabled do not receive GPOE. Verify that the even# computer receives this policy and the odd# computer does not.

POST-LAB CLEANUP

- Enable the Computer Browser and Task Scheduler services on the even# computer.

1. On the even# computer, log on as the default administrator of the domain*xx* domain.
2. Open a command prompt window.
3. Type **sc config browser start= auto** and press ENTER.
4. Type **sc config schedule start= auto** and press ENTER.
5. Close the command prompt window.

- Remove all GPOs you created during this lab.

1. On the odd# computer, log on as the default administrator of the domain*xx* domain.
2. Click Start and then click Run.
3. Type **dsa.msc** in the Run dialog box and click OK.
4. Right-click the domain*xx*.local object and click Properties.
5. Click the Group Policy tab and then click Open. The Group Policy Management Console opens.
6. In the left window pane, expand the Group Policy Objects object and click Group Policy Objects. All the GPOs you created should appear under this object.

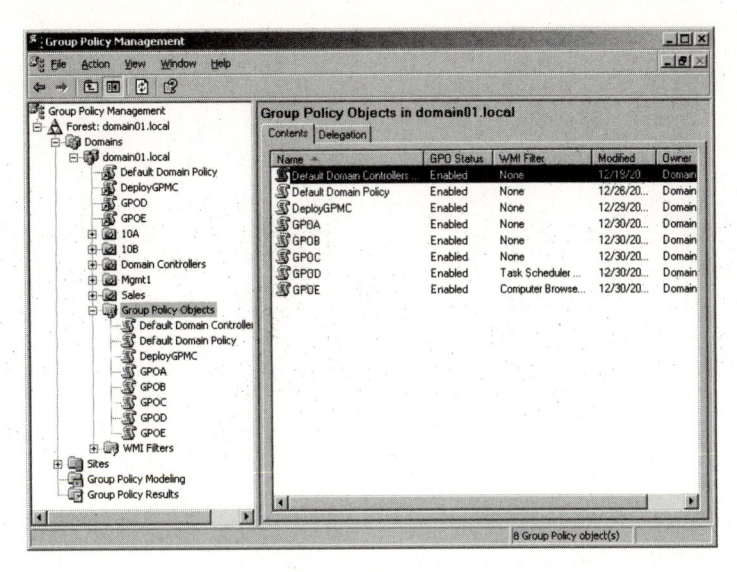

7. In the right window pane, right-click GPOE, click Delete, and then confirm by clicking OK twice. Delete all the GPOs you created in this lab (GPOA, GPOB, GPOC, GPOD, and GPOE).

8. Close the Group Policy Management Console. Click OK in the domain*xx* Properties dialog box. Close the Active Directory Users And Computers console.

9. Restart both computers.

LAB 11
DISASTER RECOVERY AND MAINTENANCE

This lab contains the following exercises and activities:

- Exercise 11-1: Replica Domain Controller
- Exercise 11-2: Resolving Replication Issues
- Exercise 11-3: System State Data Backup
- Exercise 11-4: Compacting the Database
- Exercise 11-5: Authoritative Restore
- Lab Review Questions
- Lab Challenge 11-1: Restoring a User Account

You are a network administrator for Humongous Insurance. The company uses a single Active Directory domain named humongousinsurance.com. The domain has 16 Active Directory sites worldwide. You are the lead administrator for Main_Site. You are responsible for all Active Directory related issues. You must ensure that all sites have proper load-balancing and fault tolerance. Furthermore, you must resolve any discrepancies with the Active Directory database.

After completing this lab, you will be able to:

- Install a replica domain controller
- Identify and resolve Active Directory data collisions
- Resolve parent object deletions
- Compact the Active Directory database
- Perform an authoritative restore

Estimated lesson time: 190 minutes

> **NOTE** In this lab you will see the characters xx, yy, and zz. These directions assume that you are working on computers configured in pairs and that each computer has a number. One number is odd and the other number is even. For example, Computer01 is the odd# computer and Computer02 is the even# computer. When you see xx, substitute the unique number assigned to the odd# computer. When you see yy, substitute the unique number assigned to the even# computer. When you see zz, substitute the number assigned to the computer at which you are working, either odd or even.
>
> Whenever you see the Manage Your Server page appear in this lab, select the Don't Display This Page At Logon check box and close the Manage Your Server page.

LAB DEPENDENCIES

In order to complete this lab, you must be sure that the following is done:

- The even# computer must be configured to use the odd# computer as its Preferred DNS Server, as explained in Lab Exercise 1-4.
- Active Directory is installed on the odd# computer. Lab Exercise 2-1 covers the installation of Active Directory on the odd# computer.
- The even# computer must be a member of the odd# computer's domain, as shown in Lab Exercise 2-3.
- Support Tools must be installed, as described in Lab Exercise 3-1.
- The even# computer must not be a domain controller for the child domain. If the even# computer is a domain controller for the child domain, you must demote it as shown in Lab Exercise 7-1.

EXERCISE 11-1: REPLICA DOMAIN CONTROLLER

Estimated completion time: 20 minutes

You want to improve fault tolerance and performance on your domain. You decide to install a replica domain controller.

To install a replica domain controller:

1. On the even# computer, log on as the default administrator of the domain*xx* domain.
2. Run Dcpromo. To run Dcpromo, click Start, click Run, type **dcpromo**, and press ENTER.

3. The Welcome To The Active Directory Installation Wizard appears. Click Next to proceed with the Active Directory installation.

4. On the Operating System Compatibility page, click Next.

5. On the Domain Controller Type page, select the Additional Domain Controller For An Existing Domain radio button, and then click Next.

6. On the Network Credentials page, enter the username and password for the default administrator of the domain*xx* domain, and then click Next.

7. On the Additional Domain Controller page domain*xx*.local should already be listed as the domain name; click Next.

8. On the Database And Log Folders page, click Next. This leaves the log files and database in their default location.

   NOTE Although not done in this course, you should try to separate the operating system files, Active Directory database, and log files. When possible, place the operating system files, Active Directory database files, and log files on separate drives. If you have three separate physical hard disk drives, you should maintain each item on a separate drive because that configuration improves the overall performance of the domain controller.

9. On the Shared System Volume page, ensure that the Sysvol folder is on a volume formatted as NTFS. Click Next.

10. On the Directory Services Restore Mode Administrator Password page, type **MSPress#1** as the restore mode password. Confirm the password by typing it again, and then click Next to proceed with the Active Directory installation.

11. Review the Summary page and then click Next to install Active Directory.

12. When the Completing The Active Directory Installation Wizard page appears, click Finish, and then click Restart Now. The even# computer restarts.

EXERCISE 11-2: RESOLVING REPLICATION ISSUES

Estimated completion time: 30 minutes
Your manager sends e-mail messages to two different administrators to perform the same tasks. These administrators perform the tasks on two different domain controllers in two different sites. After replication occurs, you notice odd results in Active Directory Users And Computers.

Creating the Issue
To simulate this situation, perform the following steps:

1. Log on to the even# computer as the default administrator of the domain*xx* domain.

2. Open the Active Directory Users And Computers console.

3. Ensure you are connected to the even# computer with the console. To do so, right-click the Active Directory Users And Computers object in the left window pane and then click Connect To Domain Controller. Ensure that Current Domain Controller is set to computer*yy*.domain*xx*.local. If not, you should select computer*yy*.domain*xx*.local in the Or Select An Available Domain Controller box. Click OK.

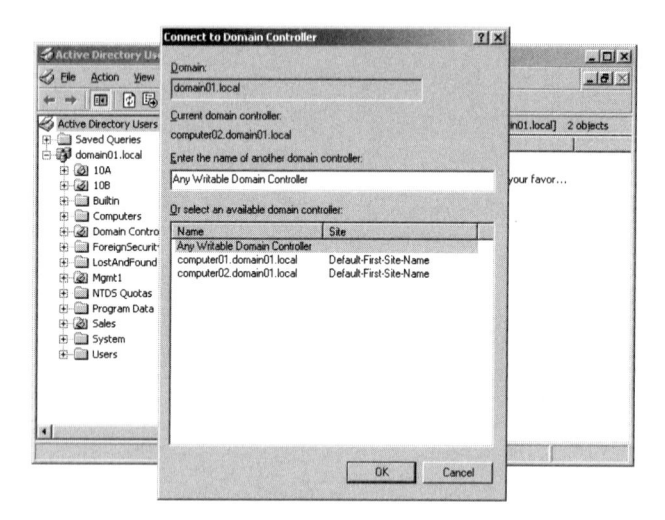

4. Create a new organizational unit (OU) named Administration in the domain*xx*.local domain.

5. On the odd# computer, log on as the default administrator of the domain*xx* domain.

6. Open the Active Directory Users And Computers console.

7. Ensure you are connected to the odd# computer with the console. To do so, right-click the Active Directory Users And Computers object in the left window pane and then click Connect To Domain Controller. Ensure that the Current Domain Controller is set to computer*xx*.domain*xx*.local. If not, you should select computer*xx*.domain*xx*.local in the Or Select An Available Domain Controller box. Click OK.

8. Ensure that the Administration OU has replicated to the odd# computer. You may need to wait for a few minutes. If you do not want to wait, then force replication (reference Lab Exercise 3-1).

9. On the even# computer, simulate a replication delay by disabling the network connection. To disable the network connection, click Start, point to Control Panel, Network Connections, and then click Local Area Connection. The Local Area Connection Status dialog box opens. Click Disable. This prevents the two domain controllers from replicating.

    NOTE *If you are using Virtual PC, you can pause the computer to simulate a replication delay, instead of disabling the network connection.*

10. On the odd# computer, create three new user accounts inside the Administration OU. Name the user accounts Misty, Samantha, and Denise. For all of these accounts use **MSPress#1** as the password and clear the User Must Change Password At Next Logon check box.

11. On the odd# computer, create a new OU named Accounting in the domain*xx*.local domain.

12. Disable the network connection on the odd# computer.

13. Once the odd# computer's network connection is disabled, enable the even# computer's network connection. To enable the network connection, click Start, point to Control Panel, Network Connections, and then click Local Area Connection. The Local Area Connection Status dialog box appears. Click Enable to enable the connection.

14. On the even# computer, create a new OU named Accounting in the domai*xx*.local domain.

15. Create two new user accounts inside the Accounting OU. Name the user accounts Wedge and Wood. For both of these accounts, use **MSPress#1** as the password and clear the User Must Change Password At Next Logon check box.

    NOTE Since the network connection on the odd# computer is disabled, the following error might display when creating the user accounts.

    [Active Directory dialog box: Windows cannot verify that the user name is unique because the following error occurred while contacting the global catalog: The server is not operational. Windows will create this user account, but the user can log on only after the user name is verified to be unique. Make sure the global catalog is available. For more information about troubleshooting this issue, see Windows Help.]

16. On the even# computer, delete the Administration OU from the domain.

17. Enable the network connection on the odd# computer to allow the two servers to replicate their changes. If you do not want to wait, force replication.

Discovering and Resolving the Issue

You discover that the Administration OU you created earlier with several user accounts is now missing. You learn that another administrator, at another site, deleted the OU. You contact this administrator to find out what happened. You learn that when the other administrator deleted the Administration OU there were no user accounts in that OU. You also learn that the other administrator created an OU named Accounting nearly at the same time you did. You know there is a replication delay between the two computers, so you think there might be two Accounting OUs.

To view the replication issue:

1. On the odd# computer, close the Active Directory Users And Computers console and then open it again. This refreshes the information. When the console reappears, you should see that the Administration OU is gone. There are also two Accounting OUs, one of which has additional characters.

152 LAB 11: DISASTER RECOVERY AND MAINTENANCE

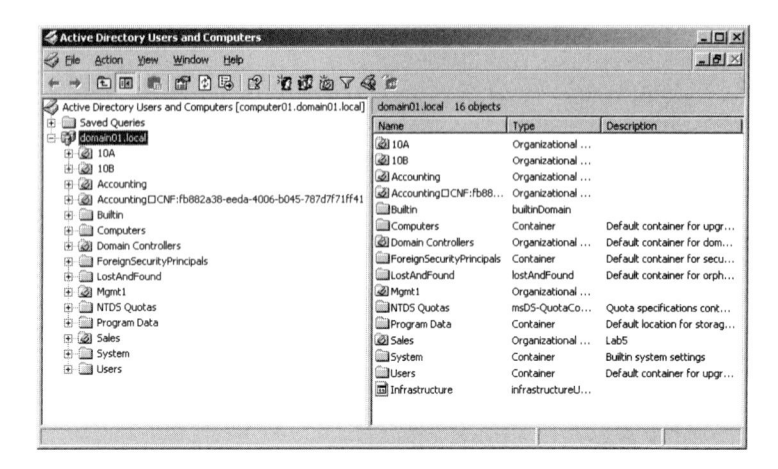

2. In the Active Directory Users And Computers console, ensure that the Advanced Features view option is enabled. To verify this option is enabled, click the View menu. If there is a check mark next to Advanced Features, then the option is enabled. If there is not a check mark, then click Advanced Features to enable it.

QUESTION What does the alphanumeric string appened to the Accounting OU name represent?

3. In the left window pane, click the LostAndFound object. In this container, you should see the three user accounts (Denise, Misty, and Samantha) you created earlier.

QUESTION Why are these user accounts in the LostAndFound container?

4. To resolve the loss of the Administration OU, create a new Administration OU. Then, move the users from the LostAndFound container to the new Administration OU.

5. To resolve the Accounting OU problem, you should first look to see if either OU has objects. If the Accounting OU with the alphanumeric string appended to the name has unique objects, such as users Wedge and Wood, move all the objects to the Accounting OU. Then, delete the Accounting OU with the alphanumeric string appended.

6. Close Active Directory Users And Computers on both computers.

EXERCISE 11-3: SYSTEM STATE DATA BACKUP

Estimated completion time: 15 minutes

You are about to make some configuration changes to your Active Directory database. You want to have a current System State data backup before you proceed.

NOTE This exercise should be performed on both computers.

To perform a backup:

1. Ensure that you are logged on as the default administrator of the domain*xx* domain. Click Start, point to All Programs, Accessories, System Tools, and then click Backup. The Backup Or Restore Wizard appears.

   NOTE If you see a Backup Utility window instead of the Backup Or Restore Wizard, you are running in Advanced Mode. To switch to Wizard Mode, click the Wizard Mode link on the Welcome tab.

2. Click Next. The Backup Or Restore page appears.

3. Verify the Back Up Files And Settings radio button is selected and click Next. The What To Back Up page appears.

4. Click Let Me Choose What To Back Up and then click Next. The Items To Back Up page appears.

5. In the left window pane, expand the My Computer object. Select the System State check box.

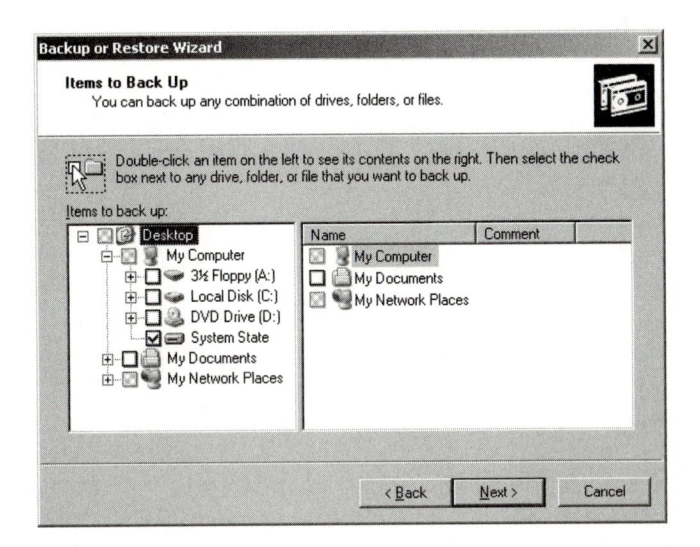

6. Click Next. The Backup Type, Destination, And Name page appears.

7. Click Browse. The Save As dialog box appears.

8. Click Save. This will save the backup file with the name Backup.bkf in the My Documents folder.

9. Click Next. The Completing The Backup Or Restore Wizard page appears.

   NOTE When backing up production servers, you typically use the Advanced button, select a backup type, and select other options, such as Verify Data After Backup. In this exercise, using the Advanced options is not necessary.

10. Click Finish to begin backing up the System State data. The Backup Progress dialog box appears. The backup process takes several minutes to complete.

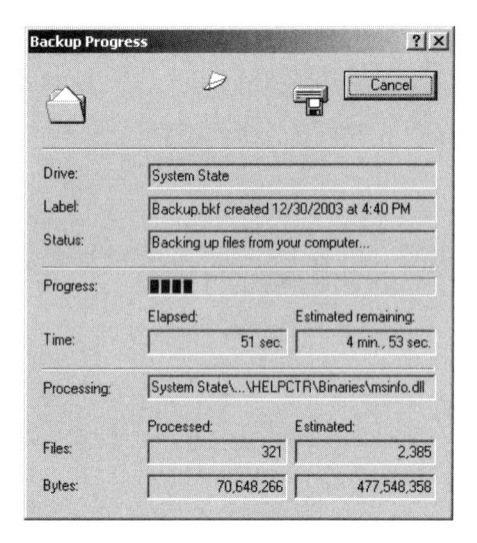

11. When the process is complete, click Close.

EXERCISE 11-4: COMPACTING THE DATABASE

Estimated completion time: 30 minutes

You want to reduce the space that Active Directory occupies on your domain controller.

NOTE *You can perform this exercise on either computer or both.*

To compact the Active Directory database offline:

1. Restart the computer. During the startup process, as soon as Windows Server 2003 starts to load, press the F8 key. The Windows Advanced Options Menu appears.

    NOTE *If you have a Windows Server 2003 CD in your CD/DVD drive, you may want to remove it from the drive. Doing so will make it easier to access the Windows Advanced Options Menu. Otherwise, you will have to press the F8 key immediately after the Press Any Key To Boot From CD message disappears.*

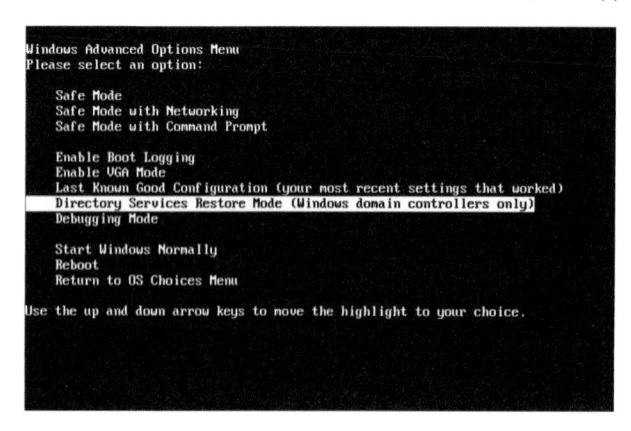

2. Select the Directory Services Restore Mode (Windows Domain Controllers Only) option and press ENTER.

   NOTE *If you see the Please Select The Operating System To Start screen, you should have only one option, Windows Server 2003, Enterprise. Press Enter. The computer loads Windows Server 2003 in Safe Mode with the Active Directory database offline.*

3. Once Windows starts, log on using the Active Directory restore mode administrator name and password. The administrator username should be Administrator and the password should be **MSPress#1**.

4. A Desktop warning message appears indicating that Windows is running in Safe mode. Confirm that you understand this by clicking OK.

5. Open a command prompt window, type **ntdsutil** and press ENTER. The Ntdsutil prompt is displayed.

6. Type **files** and press ENTER. The File Maintenance prompt is displayed.

7. Type **?** and press ENTER. Notice that you have several options at this prompt. You can check the Active Directory database integrity, move the database, and move the database log files.

8. Type **info** and press ENTER. This command displays the current location of the Active Directory database (ntds.dit), the backup directory, and the log files directory.

9. In order to perform offline compaction of the database, type **compact to c:** and press ENTER. The database is compacted and you are given directions on how to replace the existing database.

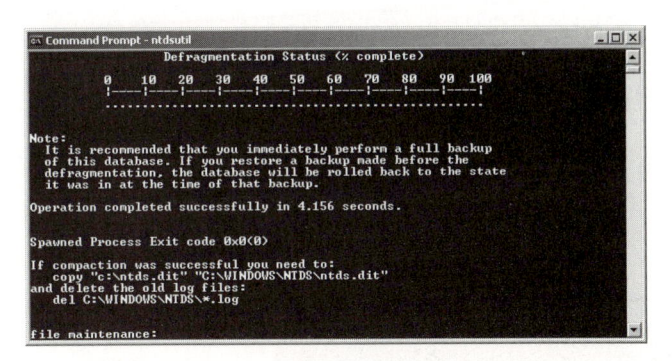

   Type **quit** and press ENTER. The Ntdsutil prompt appears. Type **quit** again and press ENTER. You are returned to the command prompt.

10. Type **move %systemroot%\ntds\ntds.dit c:\ntds.old** and press ENTER. This saves your old Active Directory database, in case you have trouble with the newly compacted database. You can delete this copy after you verify that the newly compacted Active Directory database loads correctly after you restart the computer. Otherwise, you can use the ntds.old file to replace the compacted database.

11. Type **move %systemroot%\ntds*.log c:** and press ENTER. This command moves the former Active Directory database log files to the C: drive.

12. Type **move c:\ntds.dit %systemroot%\ntds\ntds.dit** and press ENTER. This command places the newly compacted database in the appropriate location to load when you restart the computer.

13. Type **dir c:\ntds.old** and press ENTER. Statistics on the previous copy of the Active Directory database are displayed.

14. Type **dir %systemroot%\ntds\ntds.dit** and press ENTER. Statistics on the newly compacted Active Directory database are displayed. Compare the size of the ntds.old file to the size of the ntds.dit file.

    NOTE *You may not see a size difference between the compacted file and the original file. This is due to the fact that the database hasn't had a chance to become fragmented. On a computer that hosts an Active Directory database that experiences a large number of changes, you could presumably reduce the amount of space that the Active Directory database occupied with the compacting process.*

15. You have now successfully compacted the Active Directory database. Type **exit** and press ENTER.

16. Restart the computer. Allow the system to start up normally.

17. If the computer starts properly without errors, log on as the default administrator of the domain*xx* domain. Open a command prompt window. Type **del c:\ntds.old c:\res*.log c:\edb*.log** and press Enter. This will delete the old Active Directory database and log files. Close the command prompt window.

    NOTE *If the Active Directory database doesn't load properly when you restart the computer, you will need to restart in Directory Services Restore Mode. You will then open a command prompt and type* **move c:\ntds.old %systemroot%\ntds\ntds.dit***, which will replace the compacted copy of the database with the old copy of the Active Directory database. You will also need to copy the old log files from the C: drive to the %systemroot%\ntds folder.*

EXERCISE 11-5: AUTHORITATIVE RESTORE

Estimated completion time: 30 minutes

You accidentally delete an organizational unit (OU) and all of its user accounts. You want to restore the OU using an authoritative restore.

NOTE *You can perform this exercise from either computer, but not both. You must first complete Lab Exercise 11-3 on the computer you select to use for this exercise.*

To practice using the authoritative restore process:

1. Ensure that you are logged on as the default administrator of the domain*xx* domain.

2. Open Active Directory Users And Computers.

3. Delete the Administration OU. Since there are objects in this container, you must confirm the deletion by clicking Yes when you receive the Active Directory warning message.

4. Close Active Directory Users And Computers.

5. Restart the computer. During the startup process, as soon as Windows Server 2003 starts to load, press the F8 key. The Windows Advanced Options Menu appears.

6. Select the Directory Services Restore Mode (Windows Domain Controllers Only) option and press ENTER. The computer loads Windows Server 2003 in Safe Mode with the Active Directory database offline.

   NOTE If you see the Please Select The Operating System To Start screen, you should have only one option, Windows Server 2003, Enterprise. Press Enter. The computer loads Windows Server 2003 in Safe Mode with the Active Directory database offline.

7. Log on using the Active Directory Restore Mode administrator username and password. The administrator username should be Administrator and the password should be **MSPress#1**.

8. A Desktop warning message appears indicating that Windows is running in Safe Mode. Confirm that you understand this by clicking OK.

9. Click Start, point to All Programs, Accessories, System Tools, and then click Backup. The Backup Or Restore Wizard appears.

   NOTE If you see a Backup Utility window instead of the Backup Or Restore Wizard, you are running in Advanced Mode. To switch to Wizard Mode, click the Wizard Mode link on the Welcome tab.

10. Click Next. The Backup Or Restore page appears.

11. Select the Restore Files And Settings radio button and click Next. The What To Restore page appears.

12. Expand the File and Backup.bkf objects in the Items To Restore pane.

13. Select the System State check box.

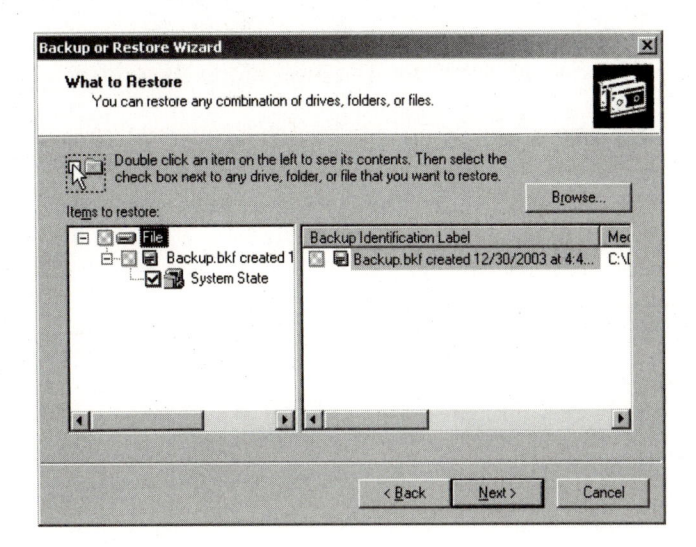

14. Click Next. The Completing The Backup Or Restore Wizard page appears.

15. Click Finish. A Warning appears. Read the warning that states that the current System State data will be overwritten unless restored to an alternate location. Click OK. The restore process begins and will take several minutes.

16. When the process is complete, click Close. A Backup Utility message box appears asking to restart the computer. Click No.

    NOTE If you were performing a non-authoritative restore, you could restart at this point. However, you are trying to perform an authoritative restore, so you should not restart the computer.

17. Open a command prompt window, type **ntdsutil** and press ENTER. The Ntdsutil prompt is displayed.

18. Type **authoritative restore** and press ENTER. The Authoritative Restore prompt is displayed.

19. Type **?** and press ENTER. Note the available options.

20. Type **restore subtree ou=Administration,dc=domain*xx*,dc=local** and press ENTER. The Authoritive Restore Confirmation Dialog box appears.

21. Click Yes. The process may take a couple of minutes to complete. You should see a message stating that the authoritative restore completed successfully.

22. Type **quit** and press ENTER. Type **quit** again and press ENTER. You are returned to the command prompt.

23. Close the command prompt window and restart the computer.

24. Log on to the computer as the default administrator of the domain*xx* domain.

25. Open Active Directory Users And Computers. The Administration OU should be visible in the console. Click the Administration OU to display its contents.

    NOTE If you did not perform an authoritative restore, the Administration OU might reappear for a short period, but the replication process would eventually remove it from the domain because the other domain controller would have the removal marked as a more recent change.

    QUESTION Were the Denise, Misty, and Samantha user accounts restored with the Administration OU?

26. Close the Active Directory Users And Computers console.

LAB REVIEW QUESTIONS

Estimated completion time: 15 minutes
1. In your words, describe what you learned during this lab.
2. If you wanted to restore the entire Active Directory database authoritatively, what command in Ntdsutil do you use instead of restore subtree?
3. In order to perform an authoritative restore, what startup option must you select?
4. When performing an authoritative restore, in what mode do you restore your System State data? What tool do you run immediately after the restore?
5. In order to compact the Active Directory database manually, what startup option must you select?
6. How do you access the Windows Advanced Option Menu?
7. What command do you type at the File Maintenance prompt if you want to compact your Active Directory database to a directory named Database in the root of the C: drive?

LAB CHALLENGE 11-1: RESTORING A USER ACCOUNT

Estimated completion time: 30 minutes
You delete the Misty user account and later realize that you needed this account. You want to bring back that user account using an authoritative restore. Use the System State backup performed in Lab Exercise 11-3 to restore the Misty user account. Verify the account is restored to the Administration OU.

POST-LAB CLEANUP

Estimated completion time: 20 minutes
Demote the replica domain controller using Dcpromo.

1. On the even# computer, log on as the default administrator of the domain*xx* domain.
2. Click Start, click Run, type **dcpromo** in the Run dialog box, and click OK. The Active Directory Installation Wizard opens.
3. Click Next. The Remove Active Directory page is displayed. Don't change anything here. Leave the This Server Is The Last Domain Controller In The Domain check box cleared.
4. Click Next. The Administrator Password page appears. Enter a password of **MSPress#1** in the New Administrator Password and Confirm Password text boxes.
5. Click Next. The Summary page is displayed. Confirm your selections.

6. Click Next. The removal of Active Directory begins. This process will take several minutes. When the process is complete, the Completing The Active Directory Installation Wizard page is displayed.

7. Click Finish. The Active Directory Installation Wizard message appears asking you to restart the computer.

8. Click Restart Now to complete the process.

LAB 12
INTEGRATION AND MIGRATION

This lab contains the following exercises and activities:

- Exercise 12-1: Installing a New Forest
- Exercise 12-2: Creating Cross-forest Trusts
- Exercise 12-3: Using Active Directory Migration Tool to Migrate Users
- Lab Review Questions
- Lab Challenge 12-1: Migrating Users Between Forests
- Lab Challenge 12-2: Migrating Computers Between Forests

You are network administrator for Coho Vineyard, which has a single Active Directory domain named cohovineyard.com. There are three domain controllers in the domain. All domain controllers run Windows Server 2003, Enterprise Edition.

Your company has recently acquired another company named Coho Winery. Coho Winery has an Active Directory domain named cohowinery.com. This domain has two domain controllers and they both run Windows Server 2003, Enterprise Edition. You must migrate all of the users and computers from the Coho Winery domain to the Coho Vineyard domain.

After completing this lab, you will be able to:

- Install a new domain controller into a new forest
- Configure conditional forwarding
- Create cross-forest trusts
- Migrate users and computers between domains in different forests
- Migrate user passwords
- Maintain SID History during migrations

Estimated lesson time: 170 minutes

NOTE In this lab you will see the characters xx, yy, and zz. These directions assume that you are working on computers configured in pairs and that each computer has a number. One number is odd and the other number is even. For example, Computer01 is the odd# computer and Computer02 is the even# computer. When you see xx, substitute the unique number assigned to the odd# computer. When you see yy, substitute the unique number assigned to the even# computer. When you see zz, substitute the number assigned to the computer at which you are working, either odd or even.

Whenever you see the Manage Your Server page during this lab, select the Don't Display This Page At Logon check box and close the Manage Your Server Page.

LAB DEPENDENCIES

In order to complete this lab, you must be sure that the following is done:

- Active Directory is installed on the odd# computer. Lab Exercise 2-1 covers the installation of Active Directory on the odd# computer.
- Support Tools must be installed, as described in Lab Exercise 3-1.
- Users have the right to log on to domain controllers. Lab Exercise 4-1 explains how to complete this configuration.
- The functional level of domainxx.local must be Windows 2000 native, which is described in Lab Exercise 4-2.

EXERCISE 12-1: INSTALLING A NEW FOREST

Estimated completion time: 20 minutes

NOTE The directions in this exercise require the student to install an Active Directory structure manually. If you want to save the students 5-10 minutes of time, you may allow them to use an answer file. There are answer files for this installation on the Student CD-ROM in the Lab Manual\Lab12 folder.

In this exercise you must install a new forest on the even# computer. This allows you to simulate the two-forest configuration in the scenario at the beginning of this lab.

1. On the even# computer, log on as the default administrator of the domain*xx* domain.

2. Configure the even# computer to use 127.0.0.1 as its Preferred DNS Server. The following figure shows an example of the settings for Computer02. If you require additional instructions on reconfiguring DNS client settings, reference Lab Exercise 1-4.

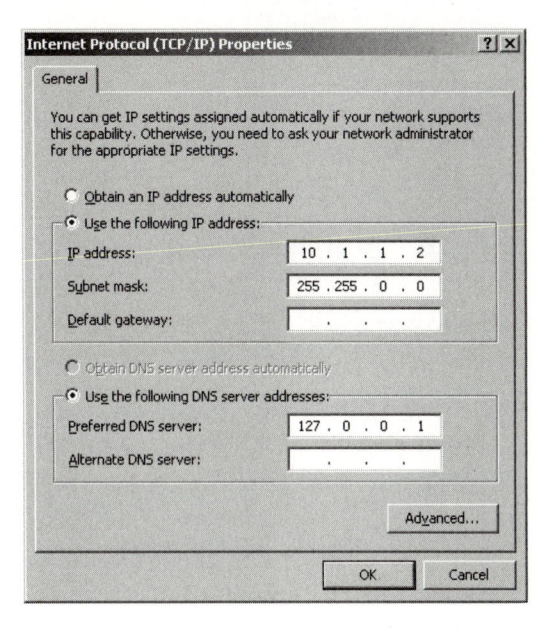

3. Start the Active Directory Installation Wizard. Click Start, click Run, type **dcpromo** into the Run dialog box and press ENTER.

4. The Welcome To The Active Directory Installation Wizard appears. Click Next to proceed with Active Directory installation.

5. On the Operating System Compatibility page, click Next.

6. On the Domain Controller Type page, ensure that Domain Controller For A New Domain is selected, and then click Next.

7. On the Create New Domain page, ensure that Domain In A New Forest is selected, and then click Next.

8. On the New Domain Name page in the Full DNS Name For New Domain box, type **domain*yy*.local,** and click Next.

9. After a few moments, the NetBIOS Domain Name page appears. Use the default NetBIOS name (DOMAIN*yy*), and click Next.

10. On the Database And Log Folders page, click Next. This leaves the log files and database in their default locations.

11. On the Shared System Volume page, leave the default settings in place. Click Next.

12. On the DNS Registration Diagnostics page, view the details of the diagnostic test. Then, ensure that the Install And Configure The DNS Server On This Computer And Set This Computer To Use This DNS Server As Its Preferred DNS Server radio button is selected. Click Next to continue the installation.

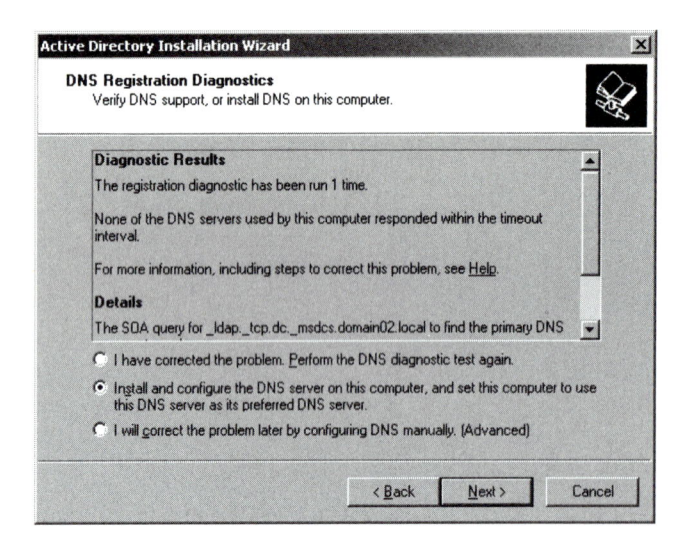

13. On the Permissions page, click Next to accept the default permissions setting.

14. On the Directory Services Restore Mode Administrator Password page, type **MSPress#1** as the Restore Mode password. Confirm the password by typing it again, and then click Next to proceed with the Active Directory installation.

15. Review the Summary page, and then click Next to install Active Directory. If you do not have the Windows Server 2003 CD in your CD/DVD drive, you will be asked to insert it during the installation.

16. When the Completing The Active Directory Installation Wizard page appears, click Finish, and then click Restart Now. The computer restarts.

EXERCISE 12-2: CREATING CROSS-FOREST TRUSTS

Estimated completion time: 30 minutes

You must create a cross-forest trust so that you can migrate accounts from one domain to the other. In this exercise, both computers are used to create trusts so that accounts can be migrated both ways.

Conditional Forwarding on Odd# Computer for Domain*yy*.local

You need to ensure that domain*xx*.local DNS servers can resolve queries for resources in domain*yy*.local. To make this work, you must configure conditional forwarding from the DNS server of domain*xx*.local to the DNS server of domain*yy*.local for all queries concerning domain*yy*.local.

To configure conditional forwarding on the odd# computer:

1. On the odd# computer, log on as the default administrator of the domain*xx* domain.

2. Click Start, point to Administrative Tools, and then click DNS. The DNS Management Console appears.

3. In the left window pane, expand the COMPUTER*xx* object and then select the COMPUTER*xx* object.

4. Right-click COMPUTER*xx* and then click Properties. The COMPUTER*xx* Properties dialog box appears.

5. Click the Forwarders tab and then click New. The New Forwarder dialog box appears.

6. In the DNS Domain text box, type **domain*yy*.local** and click OK.

7. In the COMPUTER*xx* Properties dialog box, ensure that domain*yy*.local is selected in the DNS Domain box. Under Selected Domain's Forwarder IP Address List, type **10.1.1.*y*** into the text box and then click Add. The following figure illustrates the proper settings for Computer05.

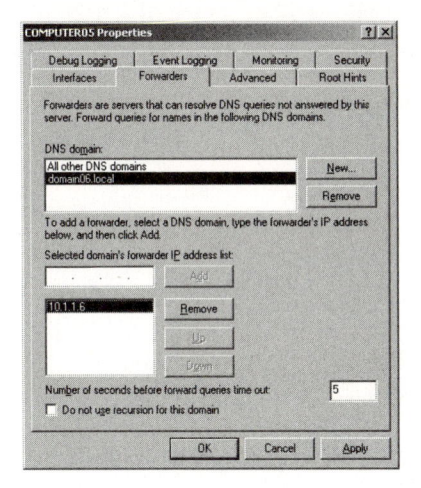

8. Click OK.

9. Close the DNS Management Console.

Conditional Forwarding on Even# Computer for Domain*xx*.local

You need to ensure that domain*yy*.local DNS servers can resolve queries for resources in domain*xx*.local. To make this work, you must configure conditional forwarding from the DNS server of domain*yy*.local to the DNS server of domain*xx*.local for all queries concerning domain*xx*.local.

To configure conditional forwarding on the even# computer:

1. On the even# computer, log on as the default administrator of the domain*yy* domain.

2. Click Start, point to Administrative Tools, and then click DNS. The DNS Management Console appears.

3. In the left window pane, expand the COMPUTER*yy* object and then select the COMPUTER*yy* object.

4. Right-click COMPUTER*yy* and then click Properties. The COMPUTER*yy* Properties dialog box appears.

5. Click the Forwarders tab, and then click New. The New Forwarder dialog box appears.

6. In the DNS Domain text box, type **domain*xx*.local** and click OK.

7. In the COMPUTER*yy* Properties dialog box, under Selected Domain's Forwarder IP Address list, type **10.1.1.*x*** into the text box and then click Add. The following figure illustrates the proper settings for Computer06.

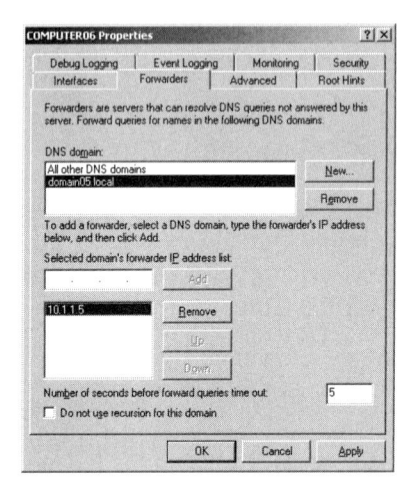

8. Click OK.

9. Close the DNS Management Console.

Creating a Two-Way Trust

To create a two-way trust:

> **NOTE** This exercise must be performed on both computers (odd# and even#).

1. On both computers, ensure you are logged on as the default administrator of the domain*zz* domain.

2. Open Active Directory Domains And Trusts. Click Start, point to Administrative Tools, and then click Active Directory Domains And Trusts.

3. Right-click domain*zz*.local and click Properties. The domain*zz*.local Properties dialog box appears.

4. Click the Trusts tab, and then click New Trust. The New Trust Wizard appears.

5. Click Next. The Trust Name page appears.

6. Type the DNS domain name of the domain that represents your partner computer's domain. On the even# computer, type **domain*xx*.local**. On the odd# computer, type **domain*yy*.local** in the Name text box and click Next. The Direction Of Trust page appears.

    > **TIP** If you have any trouble establishing communications between the domain controllers at this point, open a command prompt on each computer and type **netdiag /fix** and press ENTER. This should help to resolve the common issues that you might run into at this point. Close the command prompt window and try the steps again.

7. Verify that the Two-Way radio button is selected, and then click Next. The Sides Of Trust page appears.

8. Verify the This Domain Only radio button is selected, and then click Next. The Outgoing Trust Authentication Level page appears.

9. Read the two options available. Leave the default option, Domain-Wide Authentication selected, and then click Next. The Trust Password page appears.

10. Type **MSPress#1** into the Trust Password text box and the Confirm Trust Password text box, and then click Next. The Trust Selection Complete page appears.

11. Read the details, and then click Next. The Trust Creation Complete page is displayed. This time it should show the trust relationship was successfully created.

12. Click Next. The Confirm Outgoing Trust page appears.

13. Leave the default option selected and click Next.

14. The Confirm Incoming Trust page is displayed. Leave the default option selected and click Next. The Completing The New Trust Wizard page appears.

15. Click Finish. An Active Directory message box appears notifying you that security identifier (SID) filtering is on. Read the message and then click OK. The following figure illustrates how the trust configuration should look on Computer04.

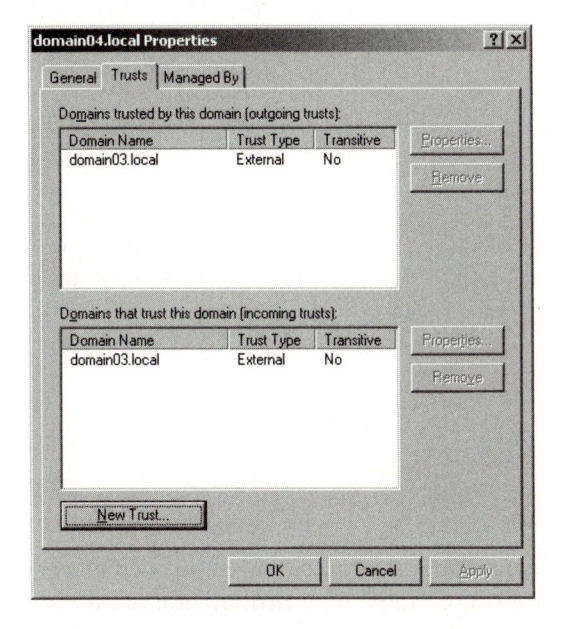

16. Click OK in the domain*zz*.local Properties dialog box.

17. Close the Active Directory Domains And Trusts.

EXERCISE 12-3: USING ACTIVE DIRECTORY MIGRATION TOOL TO MIGRATE USERS

Estimated completion time: 70 minutes

Now you must migrate a user account from one domain to the other to determine whether you'll be able to migrate larger groups later. You want to be sure to migrate passwords and SID History.

In this exercise you will enable install and enable migration for both computers in both directions.

Installing the Active Directory Migration Tool

Install the Active Directory Migration Tool on both computers (odd# and even#) to prepare for migration. To install the Active Directory Migration Tool:

1. Ensure you are logged on as the default administrator of the domainzz domain.

2. Insert your Windows Server 2003 CD into your local computer's CD/DVD drive.

3. Install Active Directory Migration Tool by double-clicking the ADMIGRATION.MSI file. You can locate this file in the I386\ADMT directory on the Windows Server 2003 CD. To install the product, follow the Active Directory Migration Tool Setup Wizard. Read and accept the License Agreement and use all of the default options.

Creating Objects to Migrate

In order to practice migration, you need to create some test user and computer accounts. You must also create an OU so that you may practice migrating accounts from one OU to another OU in a different domain. To create these objects:

1. Create a top-level organizational unit (OU) named OddOU in domain*xx*.local.

2. Create a top-level organizational unit (OU) named EvenOU in domain*yy*.local.

3. Create the user and computer accounts listed in Table 12-1 in their respective domain and container. Use **MSPress#1** as the password for all new user accounts. Do not require users to change their passwords at next logon. Accept all default options when creating computer accounts.

Table 12-1   Lab 12 Objects

Domain/Container	User Accounts	Computer Accounts
Domain*xx*/Users	OddUser	
Domain*xx*/OddOU	OddOUser1 OddOUser2	OddOUComp
Domain*xx*/Computers		OddComp
Domain*yy*/Users	EvenUser	
Domain*yy*/EvenOU	EvenOUser1 EvenOUser2	EvenOUComp
Domain*yy*/Computers		EvenComp

The following figure illustrates the OU structure and accounts that should be created for domain02.local.

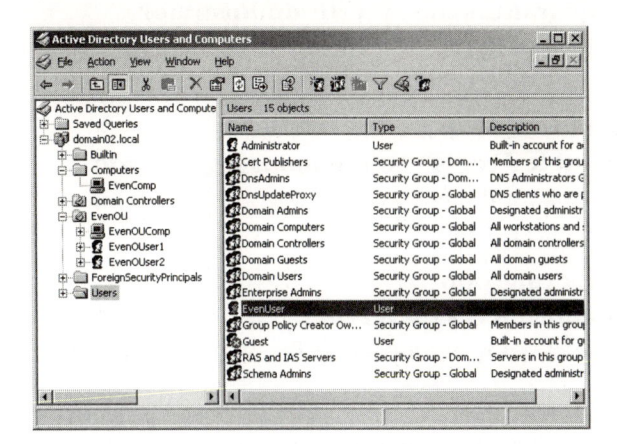

Granting Administrative Access Between Domains

Allowing administrative access to the domain. In order to migrate objects from one domain to another, you must have administrative access in both locations. To prepare the administrative environment for migration:

1. On the even# computer, raise the domain functional level to Windows 2000 native (Reference Lab Exercise 4-2 for steps, if you need them).

2. On both computers, open Active Directory Users And Computers. Locate and click the Builtin object below the domain*zz*.local object. In the right window pane, right-click Administrators, and then click Properties. The Administrators Properties dialog box appears.

3. Click the Members tab, and then click Add. The Select Users, Contacts, Computers, Or Groups dialog box appears.

4. Click Locations. The Locations dialog box appears. On the odd# computer click on domain*yy*.local and click OK. On the even# computer click on domain*xx*.local and click OK

5. Type **Domain Admins** in the Enter Object Name To Select and click Check Names.

6. Verify the Domain Admins is underlined and click OK.

7. In the Administrators Properties dialog box click OK.

Preparing for SID and Password Migration

There are several additional steps that you must perform in order to prepare your computers for SID and password migration. To prepare for password migration and SID History perform the following steps:

1. On both computers, open a command prompt window.

2. On the odd# computer, remove SID filtering on the trust relationship from domain*xx*.local. Type **netdom trust domain*yy*.local /domain:domain*xx*.local /quarantine:no /usero:administrator /passwordo:MSPress#1** and press ENTER. You should see a message that indicates the trust is set not to filter SIDs.

3. On the even# computer, remove SID filtering on the trust relationship from domain*yy*.local. Ttype **netdom trust domain*xx*.local /domain:domain*yy*.local /quarantine:no /usero:administrator /passwordo:MSPress#1** and press ENTER. You should see a message that indicates the trust is set not to filter SIDs.

4. On both computers, type **net localgroup "Pre-Windows 2000 Compatible Access" "anonymous logon" /add** and press ENTER. This command adds the Anonymous Logon group to the Pre-Windows 2000 Compatible Access group.

5. On both computers, type **net localgroup "Pre-Windows 2000 Compatible Access" everyone /add** and press ENTER. This command adds the Everyone group to the Pre-Windows 2000 Compatible Access group.

   NOTE The next steps of this exercise require a blank formatted floppy disk and a floppy disk drive on both computers. If you do not have floppy disks or floppy disk drives, you can copy the data to a shared network folder to which both computers have access.

6. On the odd# computer, insert a blank formatted floppy disk into the floppy drive, in the command prompt window, type **admt key domain*yy*.local a:** and press ENTER. You should see a message indicating that the password export key was successfully created and saved on the floppy disk.

   NOTE If you see an error that reads Admt Is Not Recognized" then type **cd "Program Files\Active Directory Migration Tool"** and press ENTER. Try the command again.

7. On the even# computer, insert a blank formatted floppy disk into the floppy drive, in the command prompt window, type **admt key domain*xx*.local a:** and press ENTER. You should see a message indicating that the password export key was successfully created and saved on the floppy disk.

8. On both computers, ensure the Windows Server 2003 CD is in the CD/DVD drive.

9. Switch the floppy disks. Remove the floppy disk from the odd# computer and place it into the floppy drive in the even# computer. Remove the floppy disk from the even# computer and place it into the floppy drive in the odd# computer.

   NOTE The rest of the steps in this section should be performed on both computers

10. Run the ADMT Password Migration DLL Installation Wizard (pwdmig.exe), which is located on the Windows Server 2003 CD in the \i386\admt\pwdmig folder. The ADMT Password Migration DLL Installation Wizard appears.

11. Click Next. The Encryption File page appears.

NOTE Assuming you inserted the floppy disk holding the encryption file into the floppy disk drive, the encryption file is selected. If you did not do this, you must click Browse and locate the password encryption file (*.pes) on the floppy disk.

12. Follow the ADMT Password Migration DLL Wizard clicking Next until you see that it is successfully installed and then click Finish. After the installation, you are prompted to restart the computer. Remove the floppy disk and click Yes to restart.

13. Log on as the default administrator of the domainzz domain.

14. Open the Run dialog box. Type **regedit** into the Open text box and click OK. The Registry Editor appears.

15. Expand the following registry location: HKEY_LOCAL_MACHINE\SYSTEM\CurrentControlSet\Control\Lsa.

16. Select the Lsa object. In the right window pane, right-click AllowPasswordExport and click Modify. The Edit DWORD Value dialog box appears.

17. Clear the 0 value; type **1** into the Value Data text box and click OK.

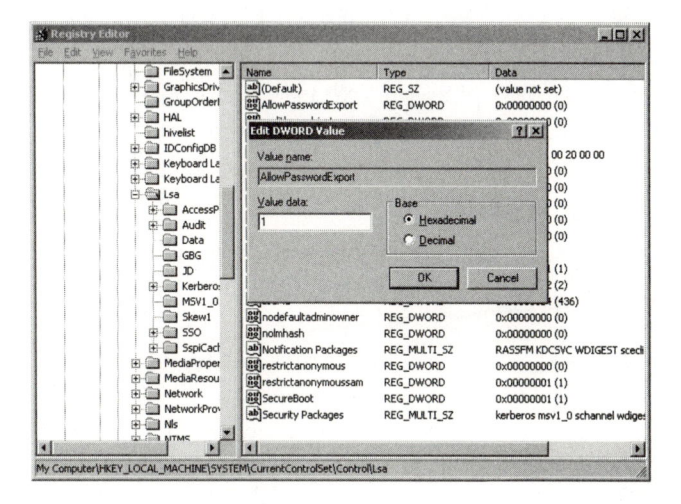

18. Close the Registry Editor.

Performing a Trial Migration

Perform all of the following steps on both computers, unless otherwise noted in the step. To perform a migration test on a user account:

1. Click Start, select All Programs, Administrative Tools and then click Active Directory Migration Tool. The Active Directory Migration Tool console appears.

   NOTE The Active Directory Migration Tool does not appear in the Administrative Tools menu on the Start menu.

2. In the left window pane, right-click Active Directory Migration Tool, and then click User Account Migration Wizard. The User Account Migration Wizard appears.

3. Click Next. The Test Or Make Changes page appears.

4. Verify that the Test The Migration Setting And Migrate Later radio button is selected and click Next. The Domain Selection page appears.

    NOTE In the selection boxes that follow, you will likely see all the domains on your network. Be sure that you select only the partner domains that you've been working with throughout this lab book. If you don't see other domains in the selection boxes, cancel the wizard, wait a few minutes, and try again.

5. On the odd# computer, select domain*yy* in the Source Domain selection box. On the even# computer, select domain*xx* in the Source Domain selection box.

6. On the odd# computer, select domain*xx* in the Target Domain selection box. On the even# computer, select domain*yy* in the Target Domain selection box. On both computers, click Next. The User Selection page appears.

7. Click Add. The Select Users dialog box appears.

8. On the odd# computer type **evenuser** in the Enter The Object Names to Select field and click Check Names. On the even# computer type **odduser** in the Enter The Object Names to Select field and click Check Names.

9. Verify the username is underlined and click OK. Click Next. The Organizational Unit Selection page appears.

10. Click Browse. The Browse for container dialog box appears.

11. Select Users from the list and click OK.

    NOTE The LDAP path is displayed in the Target OU text box. Record the LDAP path.

12. In the Organizational Unit Selection page click Next. The Password Options page appears.

13. Select the Migrate Passwords radio button.

14. On the odd# computer, select computer*yy* in the Password Migration Source DC selection box. On the even# computer, select computer*xx* in the Password Migration Source DC selection box. Click Next. The Accounts Transition Options page appears.

15. Select the Migrate User SIDs To Target Domain check box and click Next.

16. If an error message appears notifying you that auditing is not enabled on the source domain and asking if you want to enable auditing, click Yes. If an error message appears notifying you that auditing is not enabled on the target domain and asking if you want to enable auditing, click Yes.

17. Another error message appears notifying you that the group domainzz$$$ doesn't exist on the target domain. You are asked if you would like to create this group.

18. Click Yes. Another error message appears. This message tells you that the TcpipClientSupport registry key is not set on the source domain. You are asked if you would like to add this key.

19. Click Yes. You are then asked if you would like to restart the source domain. You should not restart the source domain at this time.

20. Click No. The User Account page appears.

    NOTE *If the source computers are not restarted before performing a real migration, an error is generated, and the SID history is not migrated.*

21. Type **Administrator** in the User Name text box and **MSPress#1** into the Password text box. Click Next. The User Options page appears.

22. Leave the default options selected and click Next. The Object Property Exclusion page appears.

23. Click Next, leaving the default options in place. The Naming Conflicts page appears.

    NOTE *When migrating user accounts from one domain to another you might find some user accounts already exist with the same names. On this page, you can determine what to do about user account conflicts.*

24. In this trial migration, leave the default option selected and click Next. The Completing The User Account Migration Wizard page appears.

25. Click Finish. The Migration Progress dialog box appears.

26. When the migration process is complete, read the results and click View Log.

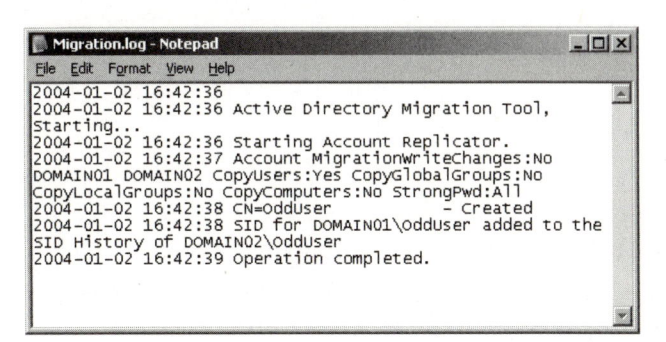

```
Migration.log - Notepad
File Edit Format View Help
2004-01-02 16:42:36
2004-01-02 16:42:36 Active Directory Migration Tool,
Starting...
2004-01-02 16:42:36 Starting Account Replicator.
2004-01-02 16:42:37 Account MigrationWriteChanges:No
DOMAIN01 DOMAIN02 CopyUsers:Yes CopyGlobalGroups:No
CopyLocalGroups:No CopyComputers:No StrongPwd:All
2004-01-02 16:42:38 CN=OddUser            - Created
2004-01-02 16:42:38 SID for DOMAIN01\OddUser added to the
SID History of DOMAIN02\OddUser
2004-01-02 16:42:39 Operation completed.
```

27. Read and then close the log

28. Close the Migration Progress dialog box and then close the Active Directory Migration Tool.

29. Restart both computers. You are restarting the computer at this point to activate the registry change made earlier.

Migrating a User Account

Now that you have practiced the migration and configured all the necessary settings, it is time to actually migrate the user. To migrate a user account:

1. Log on to each computer as the default administrator of the domainzz domain.

2. Use the Active Directory Migration Tool and the technique that you just learned in the "Performing a Trial Migration" section to actually migrate the OddUser to the Users container in domain*yy*.local and the EvenUser to the Users container in domain*xx*.local.

   QUESTION Which option in the Active Directory Migration Tool must you select to actually migrate a user account, as opposed to the option used to perform a trial migration?

   QUESTION Which messages or steps did you see in the trial migration that were not shown in the actual migration?

3. Open Active Directory Users And Computers, both EvenUser and OddUser should appear in the Users container.

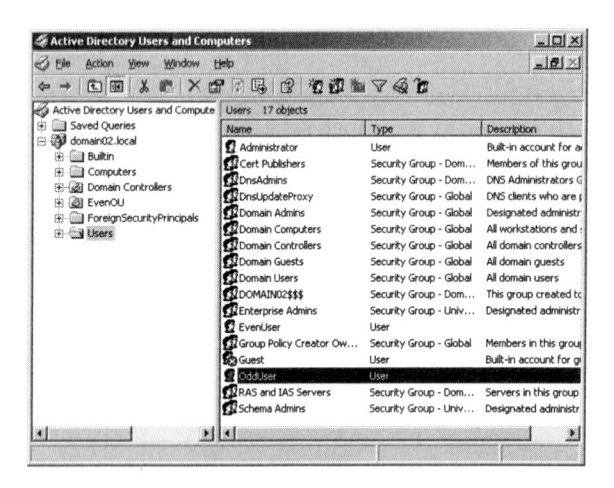

LAB REVIEW QUESTIONS

Estimated completion time: 15 minutes

1. In your words, describe what you learned during this lab.

2. Before you can migrate users between domains of different forests, what must you setup between the domains?

3. If you must migrate a user account named JWorden from the Marketing OU of the contoso.com domain, what LDAP path must you use?

4. If you want to migrate passwords from one domain to the other, what must you export in order to allow the source domain to copy passwords to the target?

5. In addition to installing the Password Migration DLL, what must you also do in the registry to allow password migration from the password export server?

LAB CHALLENGE 12-1: MIGRATING USERS BETWEEN FORESTS

Estimated completion time: 20 minutes

You must move user accounts from one domain to the other. Create an OU named OddOU on the even# computer, and create an OU named EvenOU on the odd# computer. Migrate all users in the OddOU in domain*xx*.local to the OddOU in domain*yy*.local. Migrate all users in the EvenOU in domain*yy*.local to the EvenOU in domain*xx*.local.

LAB CHALLENGE 12-2: MIGRATING COMPUTERS BETWEEN FORESTS

Estimated completion time: 20 minutes

You must migrate computer accounts between domains in different forests. Migrate the OddComp and OddOUComp computer accounts to the domain*yy*.local EvenOU OU. Migrate the EvenComp and EvenOUComp computer accounts to the domain*xx*.local OddOU OU.

TROUBLESHOOTING LAB C

Troubleshooting Lab C is a practical application of the knowledge you have acquired from Chapters 9 through 12. Troubleshooting Lab C is divided into two sections, "Reviewing a Network" and "Troubleshooting a Break Scenario." In the "Reviewing a Network" section, you will review and assess a Windows Server 2003 Active Directory infrastructure for the Litware, Inc. company. In the "Troubleshooting a Break Scenario" section you will troubleshoot a particular break scenario. Your instructor or lab assistant has changed your computer configuration to cause it to be "broken." Your task in this section will be to apply your acquired skills to troubleshoot and resolve the break.

REVIEWING A NETWORK

You are a computer consultant. Amy Rusko, the chief information officer of Litware, Inc., has hired you to help her address several security concerns. The Litware network consists of two Active Directory domains, litwareinc.com and dev.litwareinc.com. The litwareinc.com domain consists of six Windows Server 2003 domain controllers and nine member servers, some running Windows 2000 and some running Windows Server 2003. The company has 1300 employees with user accounts in the litwareinc.com domain, and each employee has a desktop computer running Windows XP Professional.

The child domain, dev.litwareinc.com, is where the accounts and resources for employees involved in research, engineering, and support reside. This domain consists of four Windows Server 2003 domain controllers, six Windows 2000 member servers, and 300 client machines running Windows XP Professional. The member servers include three application servers and three file servers. The file servers contain large amounts of data, including many confidential development documents containing trade secrets regarding new toys.

Amy has identified two areas of concern related to security:

- Many employees open e-mail attachments right from their e-mail messages. The company keeps its antivirus software up to date, but Amy wants to find a way to prevent e-mail attachments from running on client computers.

- Amy wants to be able to track users who access or attempt to access documents stored on the three file servers that contain confidential information. She plans to keep a log of all this information and never wants to miss even one successful or unsuccessful attempt to access this data.

Given Amy's security concerns, answer the following questions:

1. What group of settings within Group Policy affects the opening of e-mail attachments?
2. Where in Active Directory should this Group Policy be linked to?
3. What kind of OU structure helps you implement the security requirements for the file servers that hold confidential information in dev.litwareinc.com?
4. How can security templates and associated tools be used to help configure these servers?
5. How can access or attempted access to the folders containing Litware's confidential documents be tracked?
6. How should the file servers containing confidential documents be configured to meet Litware's requirements regarding the Security log?
7. Amy tells you that a domain administrator recently deleted by mistake an OU containing hundreds of user and computer accounts. The change replicated throughout the domain. She says it will take at least 20 hours to re-create the deleted accounts. What can you suggest to prevent this problem from happening in the future?

TROUBLESHOOTING A BREAK SCENARIO

In this portion of Troubleshooting Lab B, you must resolve a "break" that was introduced by your instructor or lab assistant.

> **CAUTION** Do not proceed with this lab until you receive guidance from your instructor. Your instructor or lab assistant will inform you which break scenario you will be performing (Break Scenario 1 or Break Scenario 2) and which computer to use. Your instructor or lab assistant may also have special instructions, so consult with your instructor before proceeding.

Break Scenario 1

You are a domain administrator for Contoso Pharmaceuticals. A desktop administrator reports some peculiar behavior with four user accounts. Users are not supposed to have the Run menu on their Start menus, but three out of four newly created users accounts have it. The desktop administrator is puzzled. Fill out the following table for each new user account in the left column. In the right column, explain why each user has or does not have the Run menu. All user accounts use MSPress#1 as their password and are on the domain*xx* domain.

Table C-1 **Troubleshooting Run Menu Availability**

User account	Is Run on the Start menu? If so, why?
LynnLC	
RobertLC	
LauraLC	
LindaLC	

As you resolve this configuration issue, fill out the worksheet in the TroubleshootingLabC folder. The worksheet includes the following information:

- Description of the issue.
- List of all steps taken to try and diagnose the problem, even the ones that did not work
- Description of the problem
- Description of the solution
- List the tools and resources you used to help solve this problem

Break Scenario 2

You are the network administrator at Contoso.com. A user named Yan Li needs to complete a report for her manager, but her workstation has failed and is currently unrecoverable. You want to let her use your domain controller to finish writing the report. She tries to log on but fails. Yan Li's username is Yan, and her password is MSPress#1. You must find a way for her to be able to log on locally to the domain controller.

As you resolve this configuration issue, fill out the worksheet in the TroubleshootingLabC folder. The worksheet includes the following information:

- Description of the issue.
- List of all steps taken to try and diagnose the problem, even the ones that did not work
- Description of the problem
- Description of the solution
- List the tools and resources you used to help solve this problem